To Mom from ~~████████~~
with the best wishes of
the author, Thelma Owens

Love, Honor & Hang On

Love, Honor & Hang On

By Thelma Owens

WARD RITCHIE PRESS · PASADENA, CALIFORNIA

Library of Congress Catalog Card Number: 75-41823
ISBN: 0378-02155-9

Printed in the United States of America.

For My Husband—
whom nothing can dismay.

Contents

A Preface
For The Young

Although this book was written with a mind on senior citizens—of whom there are twenty-two million in our country—a junior citizen may read it with the mistaken idea that the last part of the title refers to a vigorously enthusiastic embrace. So if you're young, and married or about to be married, this chapter is for you.

I have just completed a survey of the topic most often discussed in the better household magazines, after juvenile delinquency and diet. It is, as you know already, WHAT TO DO WITH LIFE IF YOU ARE A WOMAN. Having consulted the pronouncements of most authorities on the subject, from Gloria Steinem to Phyllis Diller, I've come to the conclusion that it is a grave error to be a woman at all. It's better to be a man, or even a computer. The comics and the misogynists have turned Woman into a self-conscious mess. They have backed her into a corner, and she doesn't see any way out. She looks at the pile of wet diapers on top of her husband's *Playboy* magazine and feels persecuted, or she gets the dedicated light of martyrdom in her eyes and feels like the Earth Mother, trod-upon but fertile and proud of it.

The answer to all this sociological skullduggery is simple: stop worrying. Stop wondering whether you're too good for the institution of marriage. Of course you are, but you're going to fall for it anyhow. Get a grip on yourself and see it for what it is—something you've got to try, by a sort of compulsion, like black caviar or a cold dip in the Pacific. But don't try too obviously. In spite of today's sexual permissiveness I hold to the outmoded idea that a man likes to believe he's the hunter. If you chase him openly he may turn wary and even defiant. The quarry hides, and I can't say I blame him.

You've got to be devious—not underhanded or sneaky, but devious. Modern woman has forgotten diplomacy in her urge to be equal to man. Being equal is a silly ambition, anyhow, about as sensible as a star sapphire wanting to be equal to a chunk of granite. How can two such different things compete? If you keep trying to be equal to your husband you're going to stay mad with him most of the time. If you consider him an obstacle to be got around (on your bad days) or a problem to be solved (on your better days) you never get mad at all, and you might even come to enjoy him.

Remember, he is fundamentally a grown-up child. Those loud-spoken sociologists, most of whom are male, have been disputing this fact for ages and making no headway. A calm but secret recognition of the fact—on the part of the woman, of course—is essential to happiness between the sexes. A woman sometimes finds it hard to admire a man unless she makes excuses for him, and the easiest excuse is that he's still a little boy, even if he's seventy. So let him rant and filibuster and make wars and complain because your account is overdrawn. (It will never occur to him that his account with the Head Bookkeeper has been overdrawn for centuries.) Pat his head and tell him you'll take care of everything if he'll just get out of your way and go play a game of golf. Don't involve yourself in this equality business and start figuring out things with him. Figure things out *for* him. It's the humane course of action.

I'm sure a lot of sentimental nonsense has been written about our female ancestors, those rugged pioneers our husbands are apt to hold up to us as perfect and modest helpmates. *They* didn't demand equality or even the vote—no, siree; they knew their place and could make bricks out of straw if necessary, to say nothing of beaten biscuits. Well, I suspect that those paragons were up to the same old female trickery we indulge in now, for a less commendable reason. They took the institution of marriage seriously, but not men, and we have reversed the process. We take men very seriously indeed. We dress for them, turn down careers for them, worry when they analyze us and find a part missing, and bring them their slippers if we live with them long enough. Not Grandma. She wore a flannel nightgown buttoned up to the chin and looked unassailable; if she enjoyed sex she never let on, a subtle form of one-upmanship she had worked out to a nicety. The question wasn't whether Harry was happy or not, but would he pay off the mortgage? Many of those so-called ideal helpmates *had* to get married; the shotgun of economic necessity was pointed straight at their heads.

Today's young woman can choose between Harry and a life of her own. She may be a little confused about some issues, but if she does get married she has the desire and the intent to make it work, and most of the time it does.

So cheer up. The going isn't as tough as you may think. Love is pretty marvelous in the beginning. It's all the poets say, and more. It's still worth the trouble in middle age. The final stretch is the hard one; even if you've preserved your glamor to the last false eyelash, Harry may still prefer a hot fudge sundae. But if you keep your wits sharp and your heart tender, the retirement years about which this book is written will be tolerable. Maybe, if you're *very* clever, they may be exciting, too.

1
Alone At Last

The wife of a famous playwright once told the plain truth about the joys of retirement; she said she had married her husband for better or worse, but not for lunch. There is more than exasperated feminine humor in that statement. There is the wisdom of Solomon—who, as far as can be ascertained, never did retire. Or not much.

When the work's all done, men are popularly supposed to be a happy lot, taking their ease in the back yard if their finances don't stretch to the Riviera, and their wives are supposed to be even happier, having their husbands under strict surveillance and control. This is nonsense. There's no romance in retirement. There isn't even much rest in it. You have to live with a retired man before you can appreciate the problems involved in simply getting through the days, which seem to stretch in both directions like a cheap wet sweater. I do live with one, in California, where the climate is adapted to both spiritual and physical cold feet, but the economy isn't. My husband is not only home for lunch—sometimes, God help me, he insists on cooking it. I believe I am qualified to give a few words of advice.

We are becoming a nation of unproductive older people bound for Medicare and acute boredom. Something ought to be done about it. No man who is useful, intelligent, and at the ripe harvest of his mind should be forced to quit work. Compulsory retirement is one of the most vicious evils of our age. While the government is thinking up solutions, bound neatly in triplicate and no doubt ineffective, the wives of the victims should attack the problem. They are closer to it than the government will ever get.

First of all, though this may sound like heresy, I believe retirement is the time to lay down a stern law against too much togetherness. I suspect that too much togetherness isn't a very good idea even in a young marriage. Husbands and wives needn't, of course, live in separate penthouses, though in some cases that arrangement might be ideal. But they should have the privilege of living in separate mental and spiritual compartments, because they've earned that privilege through a long

15

life of putting up with each other. In retirement they shouldn't have the same friends or the same hobbies unless they honestly *like* the same friends and the same hobbies—a phenomenon that occurs, I'm afraid, only in the first few days of the honeymoon, when they have been known to take bites out of the same sandwich. This unsanitary euphoria is luckily fleeting. When newlyweds get their feet on the ground they usually start walking off in opposite directions. What a pity, say the rosy sentimentalists. I think it's a beautiful sign they've still got their wits about them. God created man *and* woman, not a hermaphroditic man-woman. If you haven't reached this conclusion before you're middle-aged it will both surprise and enchant you. It's a relief to know you don't have to like enchiladas because he likes them, and he doesn't have to like your mother because he thinks mother-in-law jokes are sick. This new realization of selfhood is one of the few rewards of growing older.

A great deal has been written about the feminine mystique and woman's fight to maintain her identity in the middle of changing Junior's diaper and keeping the stew going. Personal freedom is a precious thing; the struggle to keep it has made history. A woman gives it up cheerfully when she marries; it's *later* that she begins to wonder what kind of bargain she made. But in her anxious appraisal of her own domestic serfdom she doesn't always remember that her husband gave up a lot when he married, too—nights out with the boys, the right to drink beer in his undershirt, that dream of a cruise on a tramp streamer.

Well, the long hitch is almost over when you retire. The children are gone, and that, all in all, is a great comfort if you feel assured you have set them on the right path and they are doing well. You have time now to reassess and reassert yourself. Except for twinges of rheumatism—and, once in a while, of conscience—you are free. The togetherness bit has served its purpose in homebuilding and childrearing. Sex is a pleasant and desultory thing, or a satisfying memory. You are right back where you started—maybe sadder and wiser, but your own self. You're still married, of course, and you want to be—but you don't have to *do* anything about it. He ought to know by now where the toaster is. You'll help—on your own terms, in your own way, when he needs you.

Take advantage of this gift from the gods—a few years of life with the premium paid up, so to speak; start being happy in a companionship without undue obligation or strain. Do what you've always wanted to do, if it's only knitting afghans, and look with tolerance on what he wants to do, as long as it's reasonably good for him. The trouble is, a retired man is likely to do some very *unreasonable* things that also involve you, a state of affairs in which you have a perfect right to interfere.

Now is the time for occasional separate vacations, to which he may object, because you've been picking out his motels and his ties for uncounted vacations. Stick to your guns. You need to get away from each other once in a while, and as far as possible; you have done it to a small degree spiritually, now do it physically. This is a kind of divorce, gentle and preparatory to that longer divorce you will face with absolute helplessness when one of you dies, but you don't have to think in those terms unless you are an uncompromising realist. Go away from him far enough, and stay long enough, for that trite postcard message to mean exactly what it says *to both of you:* "Wish you were here." Go visit Aunt Millie. Drop in on the grandchildren (unless they live in Arabia, which is frustrating to the herd instinct but helps a lot in that sense of freedom). Just get away. Get away from your husband's compulsive reminiscences about the office and from his hourly walk from the front door to the back. He probably needs to escape you, too, but more than that he needs to escape your pity. You don't pity him? I bet you pity lions in cages. I pity *men* in cages.

If you don't get away from each other you may fall into the most bitter trap of marriage—the unconscious malice of the old. After all, he didn't get that trip on the tramp steamer, and you don't look so good in dentures. He begins to find fault with everything you do. He watches girls in bikinis with such avid interest you swear you'll spend your next Social Security check on one for yourself. You won't, of course; you'll buy orthopedic shoes instead. Life is like that.

"I wonder what she does to her hair," he says reverently as the sweet young thing swishes by. As he says it he looks at *your* hair, fixed only the day before at the best shop in town, and with a blue rinse, too. You know you might as well be bald as far as he's concerned, and you feel an ache of desperation. Not only your hair is blue; you're blue all over. It wasn't like that in the good old days. You try to remember what it *was* like, and find you can't, and that is the unkindest cut of all.

So you get into the insult game yourself.

"Do you have to make that noise when you eat?" you ask him. "For heaven's sake, it's only a banana."

Does your bitter remark lessen in any degree his succulent enjoyment? It does not. He pretends to be deaf (which you wish *you* were). Withdrawal symptoms of this sort are a mean defensive gesture terrible to deal with. You wonder what you ever saw in him in the first place. Look at the man, in that frowsy sweater he won't give away; he needs a shave, too. Dear Lord, if he'd only go to the office and leave you alone!

Then you remember there isn't any office. There's just the two of you, a combination that sounded delightful on your honeymoon and now fills you with panic. You forget you once loved him. You love him now, even in that sweater, but it's getting harder to do. You don't want to fight him any more, and you're tired of fighting your guilt complex. You simply want to sit down and cry.

Don't give up yet. I suspect that a good psychiatrist would tell you that his cussedness is only his masculinity trying to assert itself in the face of odds even you don't know about. You can help him and still keep your marriage free and easy. Whether this retirement deal works or drives you both crazy is entirely up to you.

2

Come See Our Slides Of Switzerland

I have said that separate vacations seem to be a good idea in retirement. But maybe you have a husband who refuses to go anywhere without you. He even expects you to bring him his slippers in the evening and to let him read the paper first, before you have made a mess of it. Well, to some women this dependence is gratifying; they retain the maternal instinct in marriage to the bitter end. If your husband is nearing senility I agree that he needs and deserves your help. If he's still spry, that's another matter. I'm not a confirmed women's libber, but I want my husband to bring me *my* slippers (and maybe a small martini on the side). He doesn't do it, of course, being a confirmed New Englander, and I've heard more lectures on reading a paper properly than I care to admit. More of that, alas, later.

If you *must* take a vacation with your husband, make it worth your while. The average couple over sixty-five has only enough money for necessities, once the last son has graduated and the rice has been swept up from the last daughter's wedding. But there are a lucky few who have a little laid aside for a rainy day. Practically every day is a rainy day in retirement, so spend some of that money now. (Don't leave it to the children.) Travel, and not to Aunt Millie's. Go abroad somewhere. I have friends in the retirement bracket who have gone around the world not once but several times—a feat that leaves me breathless with admiration and also with the sneaky feeling that they are on a merry-go-round and don't know how to get off. Escaping boredom doesn't have to be that strenuous!

We never could get beyond Niagara Falls for two reasons—lack of money and lack of courage. I am a natural-born coward when it comes to planes. I enter them—rather, the crowd pushes me into them—as if I were entering a mausoleum. I put my hands over my ears as the stewardess explains what to do in case of emergency. For me the emergency is here and now. I clutch the seat-arms and push my feet against the floor, and when the pilot's voice comes over the intercom I panic. He is only telling me I can see Lake Erie if I look out the window, but I'm not about to look out the window. I eat the meal they bring me with the conviction that it will be my last, and I take a bottle grimly when the stewardess brings the drinks. It doesn't help. Nothing does. My friends have suggested hypnosis as a cure for my cowardice, but I'm afraid of hypnosis, too.

Ray says plane travel is merely boring. How can you be bored when imminent destruction is staring you in the face? He reads for a while and then peacefully goes to sleep. I have the urge to wake him and tell him I'm sorry—sorry about the mess I've made of his papers, the times I've overdrawn at the bank, my irresponsible housekeeping. I have the urge to call for a priest, though I'm a sensible Presbyterian when everything's going fine.

But not all the others are as neurotic as I am, and for those brave souls I'm told there is nothing as relaxing and at the same time as invigorating as travel to faraway places. It is a better pick-me-up than Geritol. I can't say this from experience, but I notice that people come back from jaunts abroad with glittering eyes and a tendency to describe in detail everything they've seen. They go into raptures over Alpine sunsets and the Taj Mahal. And, heaven help us, they show slides.

I belong to a church group, the purpose of which is to give mild and mannerly entertainment to the elderly, with a potluck supper as a special bonus. (We once had a hula dancer, but I'm sure that was a clerical error of some sort.) Usually we have slides—eighty or ninety of them at one sitting (and the sitting is done on hard, uncushioned chairs). They bore me to death. In the first place, I'm envious of those who can travel and prove it; in the second place, I'm so ignorant of geography I misplace whole continents and never know what I'm looking at. But the slides go on and on, sometimes sideways, sometimes upside down, while the master of ceremonies apologizes and makes little jokes and tells innumerable anecdotes. His wife is always in the audience and always contradicts what he has just said. "No, dear, that's not Zurich. We lost the Zurich slides, remember?" I say to myself, "Thank God for that," and she continues relentlessly: "That's Africa. We got

22

a fine view of a camel there. See that hump in the left-hand corner of the screen? It's a little blurred." "There are no camels in Africa," Ray whispers, and someone shushes him, and the entertainer slips in another slide.

If you can keep quiet about it afterward, travel is wonderful for both husbands and wives, either together or alone. If you go with your husband, you may find that being in a different country puts a new perspective on everything. You look at him in grateful surprise. Compared with those Arabs you saw, he looks pretty good—and what's more, you can understand every word he says. He looks at you and is glad you're not an African belle with a ring in your nose. You've been excited together, you've been tired together, but never once have you been bored together. Maybe in discovering a new country you will rediscover yourselves. That possibility is always cheap at any price.

And when you get back—ah, my friends say, there's the real reward of travel! The Statue of Liberty is something more than an oversized stone-hearted lady with a torch. You marvel at the width, breadth, and excellence of our country. In spite of Watergate and its repercussions, America is beautiful from sea to shining sea. It may be an illusion, this upsurge of almost violent patriotism, but it's a salutary illusion, one of the few you can afford at this stage of your life.

"How about a cup of coffee?" your husband asks when you get into the haven of your own kitchen, with no headwaiter leaning over your shoulder with a wine list you don't want. "I haven't had a decent cup since we left. Gosh, it's good to be home."

Lady, that's his substitute for the orchid bouquets you've missed out on, the endearments you seldom get. It's the best he can do. Take it and be grateful.

23

3
Take Off
That Apron

The trip is over, and at least in part forgotten. You can't remember exactly how anything looked; you remember only that your husband said he wished they'd move the Coliseum to the outskirts of Rome, being a tidy and methodical man. You regard him and the whole dilemma of retirement with a sort of desperation. What is the poor soul going to do all day long? He's read the sports page seven times, taken a nap, and seen the rerun of a soap opera on television. It's the soap opera that gets you. So you take your best embroidered apron down from its hook in the corner and call him in to help with the dishes.

Don't do it.

Your first duty now as a housewife is to see that *he* doesn't become one. On that magical honeymoon it was fun to let him dry the dishes; you teased him about looking like a woman, blushing secretly in the sure knowledge that he wasn't one. But now the sight of him arouses you to exasperated pity. An apron on a husband is insidiously demoralizing—unless, of course, he is a professional chef making good money by wearing it, or a host doing the barbecue bit for an entranced female audience who are as aware of the joke as he is. He can help you if you're in bed with a temperature of 103, in which case you'll both feel good about his doing so; and once in a while he can carry out the garbage, so you won't feel underprivileged. Otherwise, if you're a careful wife you'll keep him from too many household chores. And by any ruse available you'll keep him out of the kitchen.

He's always thought he could toss off a meal with one hand tied behind his back and he's likely to insist on showing you if he has a chance. I've found there are two kinds of masculine cooks—the eager-beaver experimenter and the kind who remembers his mother. My husband, a retired chemist, unfortunately belongs to both categories. He likes to mix odd things together just to see what happens, and I'm sure he has told me, blow by blow, every meal his New England mother cooked, all of which seem to have included baked beans and fish chowder, even for breakfast.

Ray wants old-fashioned cooking. What he has told me about ready-made mixes would make your toes curl. To put it simply, he was born in the wrong century. He would have enjoyed being master of a primitive household, where his wife planted the seed, hoed the corn, cooked the food, and made clothes out of wool she spun with her own hand. Perhaps he wouldn't have insisted on her catching and shearing the sheep, but if she had stamina enough to do it he would have been inordinately pleased. As he leans over my shoulder at the stove he talks wistfully of the days when nobody was beholden to the electric company or the canning industry. I believe he feels that civilization may stop dead in its tracks some day—and where will *he* be, with a wife who uses the wrong end of a can-opener?

Not only does he want me to raise the crops; he wants me to cook them on a coal stove. That's one of the troubles with retired men; they remember simpler days with such frantic nostalgia you're ashamed to own even an apple-corer. My husband doesn't really trust any fuel but wood or coal; other combustibles may blow up, run out, or be withdrawn from public consumption at the whim of the Utilities (a vague and threatening word he uses a lot, along with Unionized Labor). He feels—and rightly, too—that he's the victim of too much civilization. So he's grimly addicted to my doing things the hard way. None of this canned food business. He wants his corn brought from the field at a dog-trot and shucked lovingly by hand. Here our togetherness, if we have any left, comes to a shuddering halt.

But he is a hopeful, and I can fool him if I try. I can serve him any imaginative combination of canned vegetables, for example, if I complain that I spent all morning getting it ready. It helps, I find, to add a bit of sherry to everything—especially to things that won't boil the life out of it. This is not gourmet cooking; it's disguised cooking. Onions and chocolate sauce might not be a bad combination if you added enough sherry. So I set a downright intoxicating meal before him, and he glows with delight. (Anyhow, he glows.)

"Ah, yes," he says, ladling the concoction into his mouth with a somewhat unsteady hand, "there isn't any doubt about it. You can't beat home cooking. You ought to taste the meals my mother put together."

He sighs then, and looks right through me to a past I can't share, and I'm a little ashamed of the sherry, which I poured over his fruitcup so the alcohol would still be in working order, and which that mother of his wouldn't have used to bribe her way into heaven. Old age is the time of remembering, but it's tough that he can't remember some of the good things I cooked for him when we were young, and served to him with love and candle-light. Well, that's the way it goes. I agree that fish chowder for breakfast must have been stimulating and try to edge him out of my kitchen. He brushes me off and peers over my shoulder again.

"What's that you're fixing?" he asks.

He knows perfectly well what it is; we've had it for supper on Thursdays for twenty-seven years. But I play along with his skepticism, matching my tone to his.

"It's bouillabaisse," I say, "with horse chestnuts."

He grins forgivingly.

"Okay, okay, so it's stew. . . . It's pretty thin. Mom always used barley as a thickening agent. This hasn't got the right viscosity."

"Nope. I'm fresh out of viscosity. When you buy a lot at a time it's apt to get rancid."

Now any sensible man would run in the opposite direction from a woman in a mood like that. But even a fight is better than a soap opera. Ray samples the stew and frowns.

"Umm. Don't you think it needs a bit more salt?"

Gentle reader, it doesn't need a bit more salt. All it needs is to be let alone. But the only way to get my husband out from under my feet is to add salt, so I throw in a tablespoonful and we eat later at a diner down the road.

But all the while he's interfering in my work he doesn't look happy. If he did, I wouldn't mind so much. He is simply aimless and bored; the kitchen is warm and cheerful, and there isn't anywhere else to go. Besides, he *does* remember his mother; let's face it, she—not I—represents his youth, and in the memory of her apple pie lies the lost Atlantis.

If your husband is like mine, at this point he needs to be set back firmly on the road to the future. Remind him there's a lot of living to be done yet. If he really wants to cook—and I doubt it—get him a funny barbecue apron and invite some young girls over. Thereby he will keep his masculine image intact and you will keep your sanity.

The kitchen, of course, isn't the only part of the house he'll try to take in hand when he's bored. He may try to organize you. This is an ordeal only the most understanding wife can face with calmness. I married with the conviction that I was at least moderately competent. By the time he got through with me I felt like a moron with a regrettable tendency to put my dress on backward and laugh in the wrong places. I admit I'm not a good housekeeper, but I've always thought the contest between a woman and a house was rigged anyhow; few women win it. I'm always finding a few socks are missing, or a few lids have no pots; in my kitchen I always find gadgets, or parts of gadgets, for which I can't remember any use at all. But I don't throw them away, for my husband will want them sooner or later. "Where's the whatsis for my buzz-saw?" he will demand angrily. Well, it oughtn't to be one of the peculiar gadgets in my kitchen, but it is. Yet when I want a whatsis for my percolator, it isn't there. It isn't even where he keeps his buzz-saw. But it's my house, and my confusion, and I sometimes wish he'd go away and get a job as a file clerk somewhere. The trouble is, nobody wants a file clerk at retirement age. Nobody, nobody.

We have never come to any agreement, in the kitchen or out, on the subject of tidiness. I am not a neat woman. My husband isn't neat either, but he thinks he is. He has a system of his own that confounds me. The top of his desk looks like a rummage sale in a high wind, but if I let it alone he can usually find what he is looking for, by a sort of psychic divination. When he can't find it, he yells.

"Where's that old brochure on plastics? I left it right here under these pamphlets."

"And what are the pamphlets under?" I yell back. "I defy you to find anything till you get a derrick. You need a fresh start, that's what you need."

"This desk is in perfect order—or was, till you started snooping around. I wish you'd lay off my things."

"Can't I even dust?" I ask meekly. "I haven't dusted since last January."

"No, no, no, NO!" By this time he is apoplectic, so I give him the brochure on plastics, which I have put on the top of my own desk for safekeeping. Now it happens that the top of my desk is clean and organized, but when you open the drawer you are buried in an avalanche. My motto is "Save the surface and you save all." Who sees inside my desk and kitchen cabinets, anyhow?

The answer to that is obvious: my husband does. He makes a weekly inspection tour of the premises. *He hasn't anything else to do.* I have to keep reminding myself of that sad and damning fact. He was a top executive once, to whom men spoke with respect, and for whom they kept entire laboratories tidy and presentable. I'm sure I drive him crazy. Well, that makes two of us.

I still say there's more to life than dusting a house, but that isn't what my husband says. What he says is unprintable, and during the tirade he mentions his mother again; she could find any lost item in the dark. This bit of legerdemain is a point of honor with him. I guess oil lamps weren't all that reliable.

At last he tires of the game. He picks an object up by a corner and examines it with a sort of weary distress.

"What on earth is this?" he asks me, and I honestly don't know. An old nightgown? A dishcloth? I shake my head.

"Look, don't you want to take a walk?" I am very close to pleading. "I'll finish straightening up."

"Straightening up! You've no more notion of order than a two-year-old. If I didn't keep an eye on this house it would

31

go to rack and ruin. I wonder what you did when I was too busy to cope with things. It's lucky—"

"Yes, dear, I'm sorry. Would you like a cup of coffee?"

"If you'll let me make it." He starts kitchenward with the dreaded light of domesticity in his eyes. "Your coffee tastes like a river bottom."

"Wait!" I grab his arm, trying not to sound panicky. "You must be tired. Just sit here and watch television while I fix you a nice snack. How about sardines on toast? I don't know how your mother did that, but—"

"Sardines! She wouldn't have a sardine in the house. Unless," he adds, "she caught it herself." His grin is suddenly the endearing and rueful one you used to love when he had a sense of humor and not merely a sense of frustration. I kiss the top of his head.

"Anyhow," I say, "it's sweet of you to want to help me. That's one of the nicest things about having you around all day."

I'm sure the Lord doesn't mind a lie—even one as big as this—in a righteous cause.

4
Concerning Hobbies

If you aren't careful, your husband may be afflicted with something much more serious than an intense desire to do housework. He may take up a hobby. In fact, almost all experts on retirement insist that he *should* take up a hobby, but I'm not speaking as an expert now. I'm speaking as a victim. There are innocuous hobbies that don't hurt anybody, even wives, and there are some very constructive ones. The ones I've had to deal with, however, have been nearly disastrous.

Ray began with gardening. He was lured by a newspaper ad showing a man with a trowel in his hand gazing lovingly at a flowerbed. "Do what you've always wanted to do," it said. "Get back to Mother Earth." Getting back to Mother Earth is something every one of us has to do sooner or later, but I don't see any percentage in jumping the gun. And I say no man can stare lovingly at a flowerbed for a long time without becoming unglued. The flowers begin to stare back. This, of course, is a notable habit of such odd-faced flowers as pansies, but all of them look queer after intensive contemplation in the hot sun.

Part-time, for a diversion or a paying profession, gardening is fine. No man ought to devote his entire time to it, chiefly because it's something he can do in complete social isolation. Above everything else, the retired man needs to be with his own sex in an activity that helps him communicate and hold on to what he values most—his sorely challenged masculinity. When he can no longer work for his family he is apt to feel emasculated. I know that gardening is great physical therapy, and nobody should pay any attention to my belief that the activity is somehow associated with tea and crumpets. Ray says I'm just plain ignorant: it's associated with sweat and manure. So be it. But I still insist that the enthusiast should join a club—an all-male garden club that maybe plays a little poker on the side.

I admit I'm speaking as a woman for whom flowers—perhaps quite rightly—refuse to grow. Well, they grew for Ray. They grew and grew and grew. They grew in big pots and little pots, and in every available place in the yard. My

35

garbage pail was surrounded by them. Every time I went to empty the left-overs, Ray yelled at me: "Don't step on the petunias! My Lord, do I have to keep reminding you not to step on the petunias!" He spent half his time looking at mendacious seed catalogues and half his time writing indignant letters complaining that the Matterhorn rose he ordered was not a true white. He wrote letters to fellow-gardeners asking for advice he was too busy to follow. He got so involved in this technical correspondence he began to leave the watering chores to me. Now, I don't mind watering a rose if it remains decently anonymous; I just hate to give a bath to Mrs. Pringle or Lady Chatterly. To Ray, no flower remained anonymous. He had to name and classify it, and if it didn't turn out to specifications he lost interest. In short, with time on his hands and the restless urge to excel in *something*, no matter what, he became a specialist—the most discontented specialist on record.

When he told me one day he was going to dig the garden up and start over with some true varieties instead of all those damn hybrids, I asked him whether he didn't think vegetables would be more practical. Who cares whether a bean is three-fourths of an inch too long or a bit off-color? Besides, he was beginning to get coy letters from the Women's Garden Club and I began to picture him in a floppy leghorn hat and gloves.

But my suggestion was a mistake. He took to vegetables with uneven success and apostolic zeal, and he began to talk in grandiose terms of supporting us by gardening. I wasn't to buy one thing he could grow. Soon we'd be independent and, what's more, rich. Here he somehow brought the canning industry into the argument; it was, he said, full of price fixes and monopolies, and he didn't intend to support such shenanigans. (One of the saddest things about a retired man is his fear of being subject to somebody else's whims—and why shouldn't he be afraid, come to think of it?) Anyhow, Ray began to order pamphlets. He ordered pamphlets on pig-raising, brucellosis, bee culture, crop rotation, and rabbits. Then he sat in his easy chair and read them for hours with a sort

36

of bemused enthusiasm. I thought—in fact, I hoped—he'd never get around to planting. But he did.

By mid-summer I had cooked squash in every form known to man, and neither of us liked them in *any* form. He grew one cantaloupe after weeks of coddling. Our tomatoes cost about fifty cents apiece, considering time, nervous energy, and water bills. However, the beans repeated the success story of the squash. I gave bushels away to satiated neighbors. And at last the day came I was dreading.

"We can't waste this stuff," he told me morosely, "and we can't eat all of it in one season. A steady diet of beans is a heck of a thing to feed an ulcer patient." (The ulcer was a development he hadn't mentioned before.)

"What do you suggest?" I asked, knowing the answer.

"Can them," he said. "My mother—"

"Don't tell me. Let me guess."

"Well, she did." He sounded put-upon and defensive. "She never wasted a potato peeling."

"I'm not about to can potato peelings."

"You know what I mean. You can at least put up a few quarts of beans. Look at the vitamins in them."

"And the botulism."

He was a little worried then, but he remembered his mother just in time. *She* never got involved with botulism. Besides, these days we have pressure canners. We ourselves didn't have one, of course, but he could get a dandy one for twenty-five dollars. I reminded him, without hope, that we could also get quite a few beans for twenty-five dollars, and I added, more hopefully, that I didn't know how to operate a pressure canner anyhow.

My admission of ignorance was my undoing. He rubbed his hands together and assured me it was simple. Everything is simple to the executive-type husband, and no husband is quite such an executive as the one who is practicing on his wife because he no longer has anyone else to practice on. So we got the pressure canner, which seemed at the time an innocent sop to his ego. *Sop* is the right word. The canner exploded on the first try. I didn't get a bad burn, but I wiped up the floor for an hour, and I'm still finding beans in unexpected places. Moreover, the ceiling was ruined; it cost forty dollars to repair. This kind of economy is a specialty of the house, but now that we've retired on a small pension we simply can't afford it.

However, I don't believe in discouraging initiative, even though it may blow me sky-high. I read the directions on the canner and tried again. (Ray said he had some business to do outside.) This time I succeeded, and I admit there was a sort of grim atavistic satisfaction in looking over the few cans of ambiguous produce I got from my efforts. The trouble was, my husband spent all the next winter avoiding those cans, pushing them aside to get something by Del Monte or Stokeley.

After that he was contented to watch television for quite a while. Then, in a sort of absentminded way, as if he really didn't mean it, he started collecting things. He began with coins. I didn't mind too much; they took up very little room, and they came in handy when I didn't have change for the newspaper boy. But he went from coins to bottles. Chemists have an affinity for glass, and he was charmed with a delicately blown vase a friend had given him. He couldn't find any more hand-blown vases, but at an auction he got some old blue decanters he said were Colonial. In a short time we had decanters all over the house, until it looked like a tony Early American saloon, and I began to feel raffish and apologetic when the minister called. When I complained he took a load of them up to the attic.

Some people love attics. I avoid them like insurance agents and bill collectors. They are completely demoralizing. Because Ray is a New Englander, and because New Englanders seem to *live* in attics like squirrels, he had never thrown anything away. There in an old trunk were his good-conduct medals from grammar school, his report cards, some announcements of marriages and births from people I'd never heard of, and a sheaf of drawings from our sons' kindergarten days. There, too, were his World War I uniform and his track sweater from

M.I.T., darned so often there were more darns than sweater. I had a few mementos stored in that attic myself, including an ancient wire dress form and a blue potty chair that had belonged to the son who is now a lieutenant in the Air Force. When I saw the potty chair I had an unreasonable urge to cry, but Ray was right behind me, puffing a little from his climb up the stairs. And his comment wasn't inclined to make me feel a bit better.

"Makes you think, doesn't it? A lifetime here. A whole damn lifetime."

I picked up a dented plastic toy duck that had fallen from a box. (Why do women save toys? Oh, God, why?)

"Don used to sit for hours and play with that," he said, adding vaguely, "I wonder if there are ducks on Okinawa?"

But when he saw the dress form he began to laugh.

"Were you ever shaped like that? It's a wonder I married you, woman. Looks like a bird-cage. In fact, I could remodel it and make something pretty neat. It would be a way to pass the time."

"No, thanks, unless we somehow get hold of an ostrich."

I began to laugh too, then, but not at the dress form, funny as it was (more like a plump skeleton than a bird cage). I was remembering the time we moved from New Jersey to California. Because Ray needed to start a new job before we could sell our house, he had flown west ahead of me and left me to do the moving, cautioning me to get rid of all unnecessary junk in order to lessen the cost of cross-country freight. In a frenzy of economy—or what I thought was economy—I sold a few pieces of furniture, an assortment of tools, a lawn-mower, some sturdy steel shelves, and a number of books, some of which, of course, turned out later to be Ray's treasured first editions. I felt self-righteous and efficient until we unloaded the van in California and found that the movers, whom I hadn't supervised closely because there wasn't room in the attic for all of us, had brought a few surprises: four discarded tires and fifty-seven girlie magazines in a heavy wooden box.

Ever since that day Ray has been declaring that he never saw those magazines before in his life, and I believe him, though how they got in our attic I'll never know. Anyhow, they are a wonderful bargaining point when he begins to accuse me of being irresponsible.

I stopped laughing when I saw his face—troubled, uncertain.

"We've moved too much," he said. "And here's what's left. A whole lifetime in an eight-by-ten room. I don't think I'll collect any more."

He dropped one of the decanters and it broke into two useless pieces while I watched with both pleasure and pity. And, because I was thinking of our boys, I asked whether he missed them much, and whether he didn't agree it would be good for him to get back into Scouting or some activity where he'd be with boys again.

"I'm too old. They want vigorous, athletic men."

I sensed one of his self-pitying moods coming on, but there was nothing more to say. However, Ray said it.

"Who wants a Scout leader with fifty-seven girlie magazines on his record?"

He was grinning. I said both of us could do with a cup of coffee. Another crisis was past.

A final word: one of the most productive activities in retirement is simply going back to school. Adult education classes are given in most college communities. Perhaps attending one can't quite be classed as a hobby, though in my husband's case it almost became one. He began with a refresher course in chemistry and ended up taking courses in archeology, ornamental horticulture, Russian, and typewriting. He wasn't a mere auditor in his classes, either; he insisted on competing for grades, and was refreshingly pleased when he came up with an A. He already had a Ph. D., but that didn't curb his enthusiasm in the least. After a while he became a stimulating, if somewhat confusing, conversationalist, jumping from one subject to another with the mental vigor of a boy. I laughed at him and called him a perennial freshman, but in secret I admired his nerve, and felt a guilt complex when I put the Malay Peninsula in the wrong hemisphere and got the presidents mixed up.

Do you remember Tennyson's *Ulysses?* It may be sentimental and old-hat to this generation but it should be the retired man's bedside companion: "For all experience is an arch wherethrough gleams that untravelled world whose margins fade forever and forever as we move."

The mind need not get gray when the hair does. Thank God for that.

5

Is There
A Doctor
In The House?

If you're a mother, by the time you've reached sixty you have coped with measles, chicken pox, whooping cough, assorted colds, insect bites, sunburn, falls, and the I-don't-want-to-go-to-school-today syndrome, usually characterized by stomach pains. You've poured quarts of antiseptic on outraged children and battled midnight croup. You've watched the thermometer go up with panic and said a little prayer of thanksgiving as it came down. (Is there any peace comparable to that you feel when Junior gets back to 98.6?) You've dealt with tantrums and toilet training and thumb sucking. And at last the children are grown—tall, independent, and well-nourished in spite of an unremitting diet of peanut butter and chocolate cookies. *You* don't look so good, but they look wonderful. Well, you say to yourself, I did it. I can relax. Oh, yeah?

While you were going through this mother-nurse routine your husband was standing by—not to give you comfort, because he was more scared than you were, but to pick up pointers from the invalids. It's his turn now, and he's going to make the most of it. Nobody on earth can be such a steady and unregenerate and incurable patient as the man who has just retired. It's the one sure way of getting your attention and escaping a guilt complex over his idleness at the same time.

Don't blame him. In the first place, he has a right to feel helpless. He's been given a kick in the morale hard enough to dislodge his self-esteem. He may suspect he's coming down with an ulcer, and he may be right. But most of his complaining is done for the childish and rather endearing reason that he's got to be noticed by *somebody*. He can't preen before a secretary now; he can't even preen before you, because you know too well all the places where he's scarred and patched. It takes a little doing now to win your admiration, so he'll settle for your sympathy. Not your pity, which is demoralizing, but your sympathy, which is cozy.

It's a truism that most men make more fuss over a headache than women make over a major operation. (The Lord toughened us for His own purpose.) As a man gets older this characteristic seems to get worse. When a young husband worries about illness his wife may innocently believe that he's alarmed over the thought of leaving her. But when an older husband complains his wife knows darn well his attention is focused on himself. She can do one of two things: ignore him until he refuses food (an emergency that calls for a visit from the family physician) or pamper him with a thermometer in his mouth and her tongue in her cheek. The latter course is to be recommended if she can bear the strain.

My husband has been easy to care for in his real and imagined illnesses because he doesn't trust me. The general confusion in the house makes him suspect that by some weird mischance I have transferred the sleeping pills to the aspirin bottle or put cleaning fluid in the cough medicine. I am getting more absentminded as I get older, but I don't disabuse him of these suspicions. They give me a lot of free time. He does quite well taking care of himself, too. I get dirty looks and he mutters a lot under his breath, but he survives.

He doesn't even trust doctors. Part of his indignation is caused by the fact that he isn't allowed to use the title of Doctor socially as medical practitioners do, even though he worked quite hard to earn it. This unfair distinction irks him to the point where he makes up a few of his own prescriptions, just to prove he *is* a doctor of sorts. He uses dilute iodine as a nose-spray and sometimes gargles with sherry. If the sherry doesn't relieve his sore throat it makes him so mistily amiable that nobody knows he has one. Recently he began having dizzy spells and decided they were caused by an obstruction in his ear, so he stood on his head one morning until the situation cleared up. When he reported this performance to his doctor later, the good man asked admiringly, "Who told you to do that?"

He trusts neither doctors nor me, but he trusted his mother. She didn't bother with doctors either. She put a camphor bag around his neck to ward off disease (and disease carriers) and gave him oil of peppermint when he had a stomachache. But most of the time she encouraged him to fight that queasy feeling with pure undiluted New England endurance. He has a great deal to say about her pioneer spirit. His favorite bit of helpful advice to me in my illnesses is "Forget it. It's all in your head." I don't remember that he used this specious psychology during my pregnancies, which were certainly not in my head, but I bet he did.

Well, I'm willing to agree with him now. After thirty years of coping with the house and marriage, my nerves are in a state fit to explain anything from a good crying spell to man-slaughter. When I was single I was a comfortable and well-adjusted woman who could enjoy being ill. If I had a cold, I stayed in bed with a mystery story. I didn't blindly waver around the kitchen holding a Kleenex box in one hand and a frying-pan in the other. No wife can stop for such a trivial thing as illness. It's a standard joke that she gets her rest only in a maternity ward, and believe me that's a hard way to win.

Ray doesn't believe in pampering my aches and pains even in my declining years, when I have a right to a few. The cold I think I have, he says is probably an allergy, if it's not down-right mendacity. He doesn't realize how much I want com-panionship and comfort, the kind he once offered me, with a straight face, for better or for worse. This is the time he chooses to stay out of the kitchen. (I suspect he's afraid he'll catch that imaginary cold.) I'd wish he'd come in, if only to tell me I'm salting the soup all wrong. I wish he'd help me put that can of tomatoes on the shelf. Trembling in every limb, I put it there myself—the large economy-size can, on the edge of the top shelf. I don't care if it does fall on me and cure me permanently of all my vitamin deficiencies. Such an ending to our marriage would serve Ray right. I want to be coddled, and, whatever else he is, my husband is no coddler.

Of course, he's just paying me back for the benign indiffer-ence I often show to his own illnesses, because I honestly believe most of them are psychosomatic. However, I'm sure I could depend on him in a real emergency, like an atomic attack. Being a scientist, and a somewhat cynical one, he has been prepared for a long time for that eventuality. He consid-ered building a bomb shelter once, but his perfectionism got in the way until the whole thing became impractical; the shelter would have been bigger, better, and more comfortable than the house. He keeps in readiness a hodge-podge of portable stoves, survival jackets, hiking shoes, and tarpaulins, along with gas masks and a bicycle. He is all set to leave the vicinity in a hurry, if there's anywhere else to go. If I fall down a precipice or get bit by a rattler he is ready and willing to cope. But if I have a splitting headache, which comes a lot oftener than an atomic bomb or a bad accident, he tells me it's just my nerves. And he has no sympathy at all with nerves. His mother didn't have a nerve in her body. He keeps an old machete with which she is supposed to have fought off Indians in a pioneer trek to Colorado. Well, I could fight off Indians with aplomb; it's Ray I can't fight off, him and his unendurable optimism about my sufferings.

I admit I'm a neurotic, too. The martyr complex is supposed to be peculiarly feminine, but in our house it is bisexual. It is a mental flaw that grows fast in the cold atmosphere of retirement. And it is not confined to imaginary illnesses. My husband wears a torn shirt or a hole in his sock for as long as it takes me to notice it. When I wake up to the fact that he looks as if he's just emerged from a two-truck collision and ask him why he didn't put the damaged garments in the laundry hamper, he gives me a weak smile and says "You were busy. I didn't want to bother you." Not much he didn't! And he often adds, in an aggrieved tone, "Never mind. I'll suffer." He isn't an incompetent; he can take care of himself very well if I go off somewhere, much better even than I take care of him. But the moment I come back he collapses into a sulky helplessness, daring me to ignore him. One of these days, just to teach me a lesson, I'm sure he'll saunter down the street in his pajamas, and he'll be extra careful to choose the rattiest pair he has.

Of course he's begging for attention, and the only way to handle the situation is to pretend that I *like* socks with holes in them. We play this silly game often; in fact, it has taken the place of happier games we played when each of us stood

48

exactly in the center of the other's universe. There is sadness in the game as well as a sort of exasperating comedy.

But if I think he is really ill, which is seldom, all foolishness stops. He is again the center of the universe, and I take him to a doctor whether he likes it or not. He does the same thing for me. We nag each other into annual physical checkups, a must for the elderly. Age is difficult enough without the added burden of sickness.

Mental illness—even the slight aberration of the martyr complex—is even worse. It is a common complaint of the aging, ranging from simple "Blues" to melancholia. Sometimes a doctor is needed, but more often only a job is needed, something to do with the hands if not the mind. My mother impressed that fact upon me unforgettably. When she was nearing ninety she *begged* me to let her work. She wanted to scrub the bathroom, and not with a fancy mop, but on her hands and knees—my mother, who lived most of her life in the South, where a lady didn't do menial chores! She had learned that work is not a chore but a privilege. I vetoed the scrubbing but often gave her a pan of beans to string—and as she sat in her rocker, complacent and delighted and useful, she was more the prototype of dignified old age than Whistler's Mother.

We have to keep busy to be happy—even, in fact, to be sane. It is said that prisoners in solitary count the bricks in the wall—anything, anything, to keep the mind filled. Isn't it the height of absurdity, to say nothing of cruelty, when a kindly government makes sixty-five-year-olds rest?

To stay mentally healthy we must stay busy, and we must stay alert. Actuarial tables speak of "life expectancy," but that term should mean more than length of life; it should mean what it seems to describe—eagerness and zest and looking forward. When we cease to be expectant, when we become bored and frustrated, then it is we become the victims of psychosomatic ills. Doctors can do something for high blood pressure, kidney disease, even cancer, but what pill can they give for the lackluster heart? It's easy to become withdrawn as we grow

49

older, confined in an invalid world of canes, hot-water bottles, and pills. But that's a silly giving in to Father Time, who respects us more when we ignore him a little and even spit in his eye.

I don't much care whether I grow old gracefully in my looks or end up with a wig that slides into my eyes. All I ask is that I keep interested in the world around me, as Eleanor Roosevelt did, as Rose Kennedy does. I suspect I will; I have a granddaughter at the fairy-tale age, an age to which all good grandmothers return. What I have learned about the birds and the bees is a single biological fact not worth mentioning, but she will teach me better things about them—impossible things we will both believe. The other day I even got up the courage to take into my hand, and put into hers, a miniature toad from the garden. I can't say I liked the toad, but I loved the wonder and affection in her face as she held it, not fearfully, but as if it were beautiful.

She is a child who laughs a lot, even at herself. I'm glad she has a humorous slant on life, for if she marries the Prince, as she intends to, she will need it. (Princes are hard to please.) A wife can bring no better dowry to her husband than a sense of the absurd, which does more for mental health than all the psychiatrists. Of course, there is a kind of optimism that is silly and hard to bear; it is marked by an unrealistic ignoring of facts that should not be ignored. A woman with this Pollyanna complex quotes Scriptures to you, coming down hard on Job, when you're aching all over; she assures you that your latest catastrophe was sent as a test from above and that everything will turn out fine in the end, just wait and see. You end up wishing she'd get an incapacitating case of laryngitis and leave you alone. But a woman who admits that life is real, life is earnest, and life is devilishly aggravating—and who laughs at it anyhow—is handy to have around the house. She doesn't explain away trouble; she defies it.

Even this paragon needs help once in a while. She can't lift a lifetime of gloom all by herself. I try quite hard to keep my own sense of humor in working order, now that everything else about me is going slightly downhill. Sometimes I'm rewarded by a husband who stands there with a smirk on his face that says better than words: "So you think you can amuse me? Okay, go ahead and try it. I'm old, I'm tired, and we don't have enough money to see us through. Go ahead. Say something funny."

One day I really worked at it. I told him a story about a spinster in my home town who lived in panicky fear of assault. Sure enough, one night an addlepated tramp started to climb through her bedroom window. She heard the noise and made a bolt for safety, unfortunately choosing the same window, so that intruder and victim became hopelessly entangled. I don't know how it all came out. Maybe the police separated them. Maybe they extricated themselves, apologized to each other, and became friends. Anyhow, when I finished talking, my lord and taskmaster didn't even smile. He just stirred his tea thoughtfully and said, "Bad planning, my dear, bad planning." I still don't know which plan he meant—the old maid's, the tramp's, or mine.

But I did the best I could.

6
The Don Juan Complex

In the song *Sunrise, Sunset* there is a line that always makes me want to cry. It speaks of children thus: "I don't remember growing older. When did they?"

"I don't remember growing older. . . ." Ah, that's the trouble with age. If it came at us with noise and banners we would summon up the reserves and cope with it. But it is an enemy that sneaks up on us in the night, planting land-mines right and left. And suddenly we see a stranger when we look in the mirror—tired-eyed, droopy-jowled, balding. We can't remember exactly how we used to look, but, dear Lord, it wasn't like this! We don't know how we got this way, either. Women stare with bitter cynicism at the cosmetics on the dressing table (most of the jars half full) and men swear under their breath. By now it's too late—or almost.

You've got to begin feeling uneasy about yourself long before most of us do. Just as health in old age depends on good hygiene in youth and middle age, so does beauty (or what passes for beauty in the sixties). It is a dreadful day when the adjective you hear applied to you is *neat*. Not glamorous or exciting, just neat. It's like the adjective *nice*, which means that the person complimenting you has nothing better he can honestly say. I'd rather be called any swearword in the army vocabulary.

But if you can't make it beyond the word *neat*, at least hold fast to that. It's disillusioning to see how many men and women let themselves go after the age of retirement—especially the men, who seem to feel they have no further obligation to please the eye of the beholder. Women do better; I suspect a woman would powder her nose even on a desert island. But she doesn't really get into the swing of things until she has a reason, like meeting her college roommate after thirty years of holding on to a slippery husband.

It's a well-known fact that men like old clothes to the point of mania. Ray has been known to salvage a torn shirt from my Salvation Army grab bag and mend it himself, with a great show of patient indignation. (He has a sewing kit in his desk, along with Band-Aids, glue, assorted nails, and a few cans of soup in case I desert him without sufficient warning.) He doesn't even *wear* a hat until it has been kicked around in the closet and has acquired a few dents and stains. In short, he dresses strictly to please himself. I resent a striped tie with a striped shirt, especially if the stripes run in opposite directions, but my resentment seems only to add to his store of mismatched clothes. He is an angry individualist, with a temperament I blame on Cotton Mather, the Salem witches, and Henry David Thoreau. You truly can't do much with a New Englander except admire his independence, if you have a forgiving turn of mind.

I am distressed by my failure to reform him because I believe it is the duty of every wife to see that her husband keeps up appearances. (He will attend to keeping up *dis*appearances—more of that later.) Old men on park benches, unshaven, tieless, with run-down shoes and shapeless trousers—these are the outcasts of age, the men who probably don't have a woman to scold and manage them. Old women with hanging petticoats, battered purses, too much makeup or none—these are the derelicts who don't have a man to remind them that they are female. We *have* to have each other. If we didn't, nobody would care how dismal we look.

Of course, it's always possible to keep your husband so brushed up and tidy you overshoot the mark and find to your helpless astonishment that the poor guy has turned into a Don Juan in his declining years. They tell me that men go through a dangerous age around fifty or so, but nobody tells me whether that age is dangerous to them or to somebody else. Anyhow, I don't think you can set a time limit to the dangerous age. To put it bluntly, it can come at any time from puberty to obsolescence. It can come even to old men on park benches. A lot of pretty girls go by.

The one thing you can safely say about both men and women is that they never quite give up the idea of romance, not even when they're immobilized in a wheelchair. When it's patently absurd to think about a present romance they think about a past one. Part of this fantasy is defensive; when they

56

look in the mirror and see what time has done they try to cover up by insisting they had cut quite a figure in their day.

I regret to say I've played this little game myself. I'm most inclined to do it when the house seems to be winning the game I play with *it* and domesticity is more than I can bear. How, I ask myself, did Ray get all this with two dollars—a woman who argues with his check book, irons his shirts, keeps up his morale, and listens to his stories about his mother? I begin to make up a list of men who would never have subjected me to such indignities. It is, of course, a wholly fictitious list, including Prince Rainier and Richard Burton, and I often taunt Ray with selected items. I have invented quite a few tycoons who tried to entice me into marrying them. This is dangerous business, for I simply can't think of a plausible reason why I *didn't* marry one of them.

Ray doesn't tell me about his old girl friends; he just looks pleased and smug when I ask about them. His modesty is a good deal more irritating than a blow-by-blow account would be, and I'm sure he knows it. I'm also sure he wouldn't sink low enough to invent a perfect soul mate, but I often suspect he invented his mother.

Anyhow, I don't think men after sixty are terribly dangerous to anybody but themselves. But if your husband begins to feel the call of the wild you have to come to his rescue, dropping both your past and his and concentrating on the problem at hand. It is the most distressing rescue work you will ever have to do. You'll know when to alert your forces. He'll begin to shave oftener. He'll buy a new shirt and ask your opinion of it, a very suspicious ploy indeed. Up to this time your opinion has been of no value whatever. Now he wants a woman's point of view.

"Don't you think it's a little loud?" he asks, holding up a chaste white garment with figures that seem to be dim forget-me-nots, also white. "I don't want to run around like a guy at a Shriners' convention."

"Of course you don't," you say comfortingly. "What convention did you have in mind—the Associated Embalmers?"

"All right, all right. Don't try to be funny. I asked you a simple question. Do you like this shirt or don't you?"

"It's fine. You know I've been trying for years to get you away from stripes and polka-dots. Where are you going?"

He swallows in acute embarrassment.

"Down to the drugstore," he says. "I need a few cigars."

Now any sensible wife knows he isn't going to the drugstore unless he has noticed a new clerk there, a smart little person in a mini-skirt or a full-bosomed Aunt Mame who understands older men. You can get angry and hurt about it and tell him your suspicions. Or you can smile and open the door.

The latter course is the recommended one. Even Ann Landers would recommend it. No man past sixty is going to get into much trouble with either mini-skirt or Aunt Mame. But it takes courage (and love) to let him try—the one more try he dreams about. It takes more courage and love than most women possess. You're apt to remember such a hardy and long-lasting charmer as Maurice Chevalier, who was still singing wistful ballads at an advanced age and apparently meaning every word of them. You think of Cary Grant, even of Frank Sinatra, who isn't really aged yet but is getting there fast. And by this time you think of putting on your coat and going down to that drugstore.

Don't do it. I've noticed over the years that the contented and happy wives are those who don't jerk on the reins. They cleverly give their husbands the illusion of freedom, which is all most of them want anyhow. Wasn't it Kipling who reminded us that "a woman is only a woman, but a good cigar is a smoke"? Sociologists say that men aren't monogamous except under duress. Maybe they stick to one wife because it's the easiest way to get creature comforts without extensive travelling. Anyhow, whatever their feelings in youth, by the time they reach retirement age they pretty much agree with Kipling. So don't worry about your husband. He just wants to feel that he's still male, and it's good for him to do so. The poor darling isn't going anywhere. (At least, I don't *think* he's going anywhere. I've been known to be wrong.)

Men aren't the only ones who like to feel they're irresistible, either. I have a dear friend in her early seventies who told me with a great deal of agitation and pleasure that she was getting very fond of the man who repairs her car. She said he hinted that his conversations with her were the bright spot of his day. I'm certain those conversations didn't involve cars, because she still doesn't know a carburetor from a hole in the ground. She's married and she loves her husband dearly, but she has a poetic and wildly imaginative mind. However, I'm sure she'd drive ninety miles an hour in the opposite direction if any garageman of any age made a pass at her. She's titillated and charmed by an *idea*. It's what I'd call a far-fetched idea, but she's welcome to it. I think she's a lucky woman, and I wouldn't mind finding a platonic soul mate of my own somewhere, preferably in a jewelry store. I want to believe I'm still—well, let's say nice and neat. I wouldn't do anything frowned on by the Good Book or even *Roberts' Rules of Order*. I'd just like to believe I could if I tried. Don't tell me I'm silly. I *know* I'm silly. At my age it's an indulgence I deserve.

But no matter what age you are, counterattack, cleverly camouflaged by indifference, is the only self-respecting course open to you when you seem to be faced with a serious marital problem in your declining years. Don't be a coward. Get in there and fight with the best weapon you have—yourself. Instead of restraining your husband and taking back his house key, out-maneuver him. Even if he is so faithful (or so tired) that he never even glances at another woman, get in there and fight anyhow. You want to keep him looking at *you*—and not with obvious consternation.

It isn't impossible to be glamorous at sixty-plus; it's tough, but not impossible, not in these days, with false eyelashes, wigs, diets, uplift brassieres, facial masks, hormone creams, and all those exhortatory articles in the women's magazines. You may not be able to transform yourself—none of us is quite that optimistic—but you can look a lot better than you do. Remember Joan Crawford and Marlene Dietrich.

At this point you may well be thinking that I've forgotten you're the wife of a retired man, not the Chairman of the Board. No, I haven't forgotten. I'm the wife of a poor man myself, and most of the fun I get out of life now is beating the odds. You can look well and dress well even on a retirement income, if you care enough. The secret in dressing is to buy good clothes and to buy them at sales. It is wonderful what a woman can do with a few dollars and a rack of reduced merchandise. Of course, the saleslady stands by with a sneer in the better shops, making you feel downtrodden, but pay no mind to her; that little number she is wearing probably came from this same rack, and *she* even got a discount.

I have a distressing personal problem at sales, a problem I'm sure a lot of other women share. If *any* item is reduced I want it, even if it's a sari or a bouffant dance dress only a girl should wear. I stand there for hours figuring a way I can use whatever it is by taking some bows off or letting the hem down, and I give up only when the sneering saleslady reminds me they are about to close the store. This tendency to save at any cost is treacherous, so fight it—if you can. Sales need a disciplined mind and, if possible, a plan. However, I distrust those organized souls who deplore impulse buying. By middle age the impulse to buy is about all the impulse you have left, so don't fight it too hard.

I'm sure our economy is as two-faced as Janus; merchants mark up their merchandise with the full intention of marking it down again. They see what they can get, first. Well, they don't get any money from me until they offer a palpable bargain. I wait, and I win. Of course, they win a little, too. I'd buy last year's calendar if it was cheap enough. But most of the time I come home with something that fosters my illusion: I'm doing the best I can with what I've got.

I may sound flippant, but I'm not. Self-improvement, in the wardrobe and everywhere else, is a deadly serious subject and I'm amazed at the amount of time women give to it, even those with quite young children. Beauty salons are full of relaxed mothers under dryers and toddlers under everything else, including the operator's skin. Older women who have more leisure and fewer distractions are likely to be home watching glamor on television. Let's get into the rat-race, too.

We might as well begin with diet. It is the number one topic at bridge clubs, embarked upon after the hostess has presented the Ladies' Special decorated with blobs of whipped cream, which is eaten with a sort of apologetic desperation before the talk begins. Sometimes diet sneaks into the conversation even at concerts and lectures. Both beauty experts and health experts get into the act; together, so to speak, they have put us on the water wagon. (Water seems to be the only thing that isn't fattening.) I could diet quite well if I ate in lovely restaurants with filet mignon in front of me and svelte women around me, but at home the incentive is gone. I consume great quantities of food in complete absentmindedness. That, I suspect, is the trouble with most of us; as we grow older, eating becomes an automatic reflex, rather like the kiss we give our husbands when we come home from a holiday. We don't even notice that the kiss is less than adequate as an emotional diet, just as we don't notice that our physical diet has increased as other satisfactions have diminished. This diagnosis of the problem is not original with me, of course, but I subscribe to it heartily and deplore it with bitterness. Life plays a dirty trick on plump golden-agers. There seems to be no profit in being slender and enticing, even if we could manage it, so we reach for that other piece of chocolate pie.

Thus the beauty experts lose by default. But we'd better listen to the heart specialists. Statistics prove beyond any doubt that we live longer when we slim down (if you can call it living). Authorities do not yet have a firm opinion about cholesterol, which is a sort of overenthusiastic plastering job on the inside of our arteries, but most of them say if we don't stop having bacon and eggs, and cream in our coffee, we'll come to a sticky end. In fact, they'd rather we wouldn't have the coffee, caffeine being disastrous, too.

I still think the Greeks had a word for it: "In nothing too much." There ought to be a happy medium somewhere. If

61

you're struggling to hold on to a slippery Don Juan—and sometimes you may doubt he's worth it—use a little common sense. Don't try to look like Twiggy. If you've already gained a great deal, reduce slowly, or those lines you like to call laugh-lines may get beyond control. The remedy for all this conniving and heartbreak is, of course, to begin disciplining yourself as soon as you can toddle. The life of a woman isn't easy. She *deserves* those mink coats.

As for exercise—well, I could write an entire chapter on that, but it would be a treasonable discussion on how to keep away from unnecessary activity. I'm wrong; I admit I'm wrong, and I'll probably pay some day for my laziness. I refuse to take constitutionals and do calisthenics to keep *my* Don Juan at home. I won't even help him with his organic gardening; those are *my* organs he's talking about, and I don't intend to wear them out. Let him go. I'll just take a nap and forget him.

It's unfortunate that I'm the phlegmatic type and my husband is so exactly the opposite, slim as a greyhound, willing, even eager, to climb a mountain if one is handy. His idea of a happy day is one spent tramping through the New England woods in winter, scaring all the hibernating animals, who know what's good for them. Every night he spends a noisy hour in the bathroom doing exercises, though not for my benefit. (My going-to-bed ritual takes four minutes.) He makes up his own calisthenics, too. I can't imagine what he does, but it sounds like a truckload of bricks being overturned. And he looks with absolute contempt on my passive resistance to anything that takes more energy than breathing.

Only the other day he came into the bedroom where I was resting and said without any preamble: "Come, let's take a walk. I just got hit by a car." If ever I heard a *non sequitur,* that was it. But I investigated and found he *had* been hit by a car, and, what's more, knocked flat. As soon as he got up he wanted to exercise to keep his bruised muscles from getting stiff. He believes exercise can cure anything but a corpse.

This book was written to help you deal with your husband in his retirement years, so you can make that time as easy for him as possible. Nothing much has been said about making that time easier for *you*. Everybody assumes it's a man's world, and nobody assumes it so ardently as a man. Women's magazines devote whole issues to how to snare and hold a husband, but I don't notice men's magazines giving them any good advice. Instead, the pages are full of pin-up girls, no doubt to be had for the asking. Men are never warned to use either finesse or deodorants; they're just advised with joyous heartiness to get in there and mow us down. Our little foibles are treated with clinical solemnity by the women's magazines; in *Playboy* and its ilk they are laughed at. In fact, we are often the victims of ribald jokes, but I suspect those jokes are a defense mechanism. We are still the one thing necessary to complete a man. Compared with us, even a Triumph convertible is a puny accessory.

My husband often speaks with uneasy wistfulness of the biblical days when handmaidens (whatever *they* were) flourished everywhere. He has a perverse sense of humor, so he tells me that when a patriarch got cold in his ancestral bed "they just threw on another handmaiden." Be that as it may, women have always contributed in one way or another to the warmth and comfort of man. What men have contributed to women is, by and large, migraine headaches and an awful sense of frustration.

I often think how unfair it is that we have to work so hard to keep a man's interest alive when a fancy woman, as she used to be called, could do it at the drop of a hat (well, not really a hat). It's a cruel world, but it's the only one we've got till the situation in outer space is cleared up. When you're faced with one of these antimarriage moods (and you face them often after thirty years of marriage), quick therapy is called for. You can't go to your husband for help; he doesn't see how you can manage life without him. Husbands are inclined to think of marriage numbly as something that began in prehistoric times, without their volition, and will go on forever. Their attitude is not romantic but resigned. You can't go to your best friend and say you want to get out of the

63

whole miserable mess; she will tell you of wilder impulses than your own. You can't go to your minister; he has heard of all those handmaidens but probably thinks they're a misprint. And if you go to your doctor he will give you a sedative, which is the last thing on earth you want. You want to *feel* again—and time is running out.

I have found the best answer is the attic. There I open up the trunk of mementoes. That picture of me with the pearls is even more horrible than I remember, and the boy who took me to my first prom looks like a prewar hippie. The yellowing sheaf of stories I wrote in college English class, when I thought I was destined to be a novelist—well, the less said about them the better. Then there is the trunk with Ray's forgotten salutes to life, and there is the plastic duck still lying on the floor. Would I have wanted anything different? Do I really want anything different now? I sit down and cry a little, and when Ray comes home I go downstairs and fling my arms around him.

"I suppose," he says ruefully, "you overshot the budget again. Or did you burn the roast?"

"No," I say, "I was only thinking. But I'm not going to do it any more."

This statement doesn't surprise him as much as it ought to. He's used to me by now. All in all, it's a great comfort.

7
Fun And Games

To a woman at the age of retirement there seem to be only two kinds of husbands—those you can't get to leave home and those you can't get to come back. Some men are addicted to watching baseball games on television or to simply sitting still and staring into the past. If you ask this kind of husband to take you out to dinner, as you have a perfect right to do, he says never mind, he'd rather you'd whip up a little something at home. Any old thing will do. Haven't you got a turkey in the freezer? You suggest you'd enjoy seeing a movie and he laughs in your face; you ought, he says, to be past that nonsense by now. Anyhow, these days movies are full of sex and violence. As he lectures you, a bit absentmindedly, he leans forward and makes punching gestures along with the slugger on the television screen. He relaxes only when the commercial is presented by a girl wearing a mini-skirt that obviously has shrunk.

The other kind of husband is feverish with activity, fixing things that don't need to be fixed, running useless errands, writing letters of protest to manufacturers and congressmen, phoning friends, and going to parties. The larger and noisier the party, the more he seems to like it. He tells self-conscious, off-color jokes, most of them about experiences he never had. He dances with awkward abandonment, going into the Charleston at every opportunity, even when a waltz is being played. He drinks too much and says courtly things to the ladies, most of whom stare at him in honest bewilderment. At the end of the evening he is likely to fall asleep in the host's best chair and snore.

He is, in short, one of those husbands who refuse to accept the physical limitations of age, and I admit he's a problem, but I have a sneaky liking for the fellow nevertheless, as long as he doesn't make an absolute fool of himself. I, too, believe in fighting to the last ditch. Every so often I reread Robert Louis Stevenson's *Aes Triplex,* an essay on growing old that is so full of joyous defiance it excites like a drum-roll. Listen to the man, and remember that he was an invalid with the odds against him: "To forego all the issues in a parlour with a regulated temperature—as if that were not to die a hundred times over, and for ten years at a stretch. It is better to lose health like a spendthrift than to waste it like a miser. . . . And even if death catch people like an open pitfall, and in mid-career, laying out vast projects, and planning monstrous foundations, flushed with hope, and their mouths full of boastful language, is there not something brave and spirited in such a termination?"

Indeed there is! But not many of us have the reckless courage of Stevenson, and perhaps not many of us should. Growing old gracefully involves at least a small amount of common sense. My own husband speaks with humorous contempt of "old coots over sixty," and says they ought not to be allowed to drive cars. But *he* goes down a freeway like an escaping convict, and he has been known to take both hands off the wheel to adjust his seat belt. If this isn't an Irish bull in action I never heard of one! He also chops down trees and climbs the Washington Monument while I stand by in envy and horror, hoping I remember how to give artificial respiration. Whatever the cost, he is determined to stay physically young. When he gets a chance to hike in the mountains, he hikes. When he gets a chance to go to a party, he goes.

It seems to me social activities in retirement should be controlled activities, adapted to age and strength, but I balk at the professionally organized variety. I don't want to join a Golden Age club. (The name doesn't fool me a bit; retirement isn't golden in any sense of the word, monetary or otherwise.) There's something demoralizing about being classified on an age basis. No woman should put up with it for a minute. (I never tell my age; instead I tell the impertinent questioner that I am ten years older than I am, and bask in the usual compliment: "You certainly don't look it." That's a left-handed way to win admiration, but I use any method available.)

In our church we have a social group called the Mariners. The name was formerly the Ancient Mariners, until one indignant member said she'd resign unless the derogatory adjective was dropped. Now *there's* a lady who will never let arthritis keep her from dancing till dawn, though probably not in church.

The Senior Citizen is an important person in California. Somebody is always studying him and trying to redeem him in one way or another, whether he likes it or not. I heard recently about a club in which, at various scheduled meetings, the members were asked to amuse themselves by doing the following cute little tricks: read their favorite poem, bring and display pictures of their grandchildren, discuss the most interesting gift they had ever received, and describe the oldest thing they own. I hope somebody drove the crowd into a tizzy by describing his wife. This sort of juvenility is enough to push the victims headfirst into their second childhood. It sounds like the "show and tell" routine my sons went through in kindergarten. Surely we don't have to be silly just because we're old.

Some clubs even go so far as to encourage parlor games. I face all such occasions with a cold and deadly despair. They don't amuse me, they just make me want to hide away by myself and read a good book. Ray doesn't object to them at all; he says adults in primitive cultures often played games. They are, in short, sociologically correct, which makes everything fine and dandy. He says I've always been the grandmotherly type, too staid to get down on my hands and knees and spin the bottle (too staid even to lift the bottle, come to think of it). He may be right. So go ahead and play musical chairs if you like. A lot of people do, even without the music after they've had a drink or two. But do try to avoid masquerade parties in which you dress like children. Childhood is a long way away, and you can't get there from here.

In my opinion the ideal social life for retired couples is one established among their own friends, not in an impersonal organization where a bright-faced (and no doubt young) master of ceremonies tells them when to stand and when to sit, when to feel merry, and when to give the whole thing up and go home. In the sunset years, life should be, as far as possible, a continuation of life in the years when sunset was too far

69

off to be worrisome. But it's hard to make new friends in retirement, and we are losing many of our old ones. The wife, as usual, has to take matters into her hands and create a circle in which she and her husband can be happy. If this solution to the problem is impossible, joining a club is better than staying home. *Any* group that fights loneliness is fundamentally sound, short of the Communist party. At least, the wife should not leave her husband in the lurch while she rushes off to the Women's Club, a worthy get-together to which many matrons are devoted, but one that ignores men as if they were illegal.

It doesn't seem fair, but there it is: you have to manage your man's pleasure as well as comfort his pain. And if he is one of those who won't submit to the inevitable, who won't hold still for life or death—well, you could have worse luck. Just try to keep his enthusiasm for youth within bounds. See that he has regular medical checkups, stays off the tennis courts when the experts are playing, gets enough sleep, and is nourished on something besides cigarettes, pizza, and beer.

Men, of course, aren't the only ones who get a stranglehold on youth and won't let go. Women are even worse, lots worse. They lie about their age to the census taker and practically support the nation's economy buying every lotion and wrinkle cream on the market. The chemists who think up these little formulas are usually male. I can hear them chuckle as they put five cents' worth of lanolin in a lot of gunk and call it a miracle. My husband has offered to make my cosmetics for me, right at home on the kitchen stove, but this somehow doesn't seem cricket. How can I fool the guy into thinking I'm glamorous when he *knows* what I put on my face? (As a matter of fact, how can I make him think it anyhow, at this age?) I'm not undermining the beauty industry. If the value of all this paraphernalia is largely psychological, as it is, that's value enough when you're in the sere-and-yellow-leaf stage of life.

It is assumed that women don't like other women much, and there are days when I endorse the assumption. But those

70

are my bad days, when the lady in front of me at the super-market stops to paste in her green stamps before she moves on down the line. On my good, sensible days I love other women dearly, and for an excellent reason: they are my stimulus in this aging business of staying young. Without them I would go downhill at an alarming rate. Where would I be? I'd be in my old housecoat and slippers, that's where I'd be, instead of at the beauty salon figuring out strategy. For me, as well as most of my sisters, this is the very nicest sort of fun and games.

Oddly enough, the woman who helps me most to keep my grip on things is my daughter-in-law. I know this sounds like heresy. I ought to think she's an impertinent little snippet who sneaked up on my son when he wasn't looking. I don't think that at all. I wonder how he ever managed to sneak up on her. In short, I admire her with a purely disinterested admiration, and I copy her as far as I can, without compunction. I ask her where she buys her perfume and makeup. When I go downtown with her I don't try to look as fetching as she does (I'm not *that* senile) but I refuse to look dowdy. This sense of competition is exhilarating and has nothing to do with my son. He *prefers* me dowdy, with cookie dough up to my elbows, and he wouldn't know the difference between a designer's original and a Mother Hubbard. Not on me. On her, yes—and that is as it should be.

In short, Ann keeps me young—not jealously young, in the sense that I am trying to outshine her, but defiantly young, in the sense that I am trying to outrun Father Time. She is, in a strange way, my competition with myself. I was once twenty-two, as she is; I was once newly married, in a world so magical that nothing could destroy it but age, and that sad fact I did not know. It is easy to forget the pure joy and undiluted optimism of youth, but I don't want to forget, and I'm not likely to when she's around.

But I admit you can overdo this business of fighting Father Time. That scythe of his reaches farther than any of us can run, even the long-distance runners among which I count my

71

husband. He just won't give up. We have a granchild who has become the light of our lives. But when she was born, Ray faced a terrible dilemma. He was proud of her, but then came the realization that he was a grandfather and there was nothing he could do about it, even if he walked up the Washington Monument in two minutes flat. When Ann asked us to sign the baby book "Grandma" and "Grandpa," he rebelled when his turn came. Instead he signed the name by which he was known as a boy.

"It's okay," Ann said gently, "I'll explain it to Karen when she can understand. I'll have to. I mean, who on earth will she think Pint is?"

"Don't worry," I said. "I'll fix him."

I did, too. When I got home I unpacked and put on some memorabilia of my less inhibited days—a low-cut, ruffled evening gown, bright red, with sequins here and there; a pair of scruffy red slippers to match, and a garden hat with a waterfall of roses. I also brought forth a large picture of a former boy friend and set it prominently on the living room table. I admit I felt I was maybe overdoing it, but Ray needed therapy.

"My God, woman," he said when he came in, "what have you got on? And who is this character with the smirk?"

"He happens to have been—to be," I corrected myself, "one of the most charming men I ever had a date with. He's travelled all over the world."

"Then what's he doing on my living room table? He must have fallen head-first into a tub of grease on his travels. You look ridiculous. He looks ridiculous. What's all this nonsense in aid of?"

"I used to know him," I said, ignoring his comments, "long before I met you." I tried to sound wistful, with just a tinge of regret. "He was *fun*. You're absolutely right, dear. We're too young to be grandparents. I'm going to make this dress over and wear it. I'm not sure about the hat—"

Ray groaned.

"I'm sure. Burn it."

"Oh, no. It's good straw. And there are a few things in the attic you ought to get some wear out of, before the moths eat them. What did you ever do with your raccoon coat?"

He grabbed the picture of the simpering Valentino and tore it into six pieces. I was quite pleased with the expression on his face.

"Okay, okay, you win. Where's that damn baby book? I'll sign it, but I still think I'm not the grandfather type. It's the way a man feels that counts."

8
The Battle
Of The Budget

I love to shop for myself, but I refuse to shop for my husband. He doesn't like what I choose, anyhow—or pretends he doesn't, just to keep me in my place. I am delighted to let him buy his own clothes. My reason is practical: I want him somehow to come to grips with the cost of living, which he has refused even to discuss with me since he retired. He leaves all monetary affairs in my hands, a wildly irresponsible course of action considering my performance in other fields. I write the checks and balance the checkbook as well as I can even though one-third of the stubs have been filled in, long after the event, with question marks. I pay the bills and stall off the creditors and try not to look indignant when he complains because we don't have enough money for a trip to Bermuda. He says it's just a matter of good management, but he won't even *look* at the bank balance. He goes on the principle that what he doesn't see won't give him ulcers.

It's amazing how much a man changes during the course of marriage. You rather expect him to stop buying you roses and phoning from the office twice a day, but you don't expect to become his financial advisor, subject to the same bitter criticism he would give an absconding secretary. On your wedding day he carries you across the threshold—unless he's a New Englander, in which case you get there under your own steam. In fact, if he's a New Englander, he's apt to remember the budget even on his wedding day. He sets the new suitcases down in the new living room of the house he has bought for you and a few grains of rice fall out.

"Oh," he says, with a stricken face, "I'll have to get a broom. I don't want that stuff ground into the carpet."

"Darling, the carpet doesn't matter. We're home. Aren't you glad? Alone at last!"

"It isn't as bad as sand, anyhow. Sand gets into the fibers and you can't get it out. I'm not sure this rug was such a good buy, after all, but the salesman said it was Nylon 501."

So you try the coy approach.

"I've got on Chanel Number 5," you murmur, nestling as close as you can get, which isn't very close because he's bending down to examine those fibers.

"Dior?" He jumps up with a yell, and for a minute you believe it's because he is overwhelmed with your forethought. But the look he gives you is one of hurt reproof.

"You needn't have bought a Dior *nightgown*, for heaven's sake. Where do you intend to go in it—visiting? It must have cost a fortune. Remember, you promised we'll live on a budget."

Well, that's a New Englander. Poor dear, he can't help it, with all that Plymouth Rock in his backbone. But an ordinary man, say from Idaho, gives you at least two weeks' grace. During that period he doesn't mind even if you burn the roast; there are plenty of roasts, but at this point he is convinced you are irreplaceable. He seats you at the table. He does everything but spoon-feed you, and you have the delirious feeling that you can do no wrong in his eyes. Watch it, baby. He'll begin on the budget soon.

I am not a budget-minded woman. I am depressed by the idea of stashing away money in little envelopes tidily marked *Rent* and *Food* and *Clothing*. If it weren't for that little envelope marked Miscellaneous, I'd be lost. After all, life is just about the most miscellaneous thing there is.

This lack of system has been the biggest strain our marriage has had to bear. As I've suggested before, Ray is, or thinks he is, a well-organized and practical man. (I rather resent a lecture on orderliness from an earnest husband wearing one black sock and one brown, but that's neither here nor there.) He insists I ought instinctively to understand double-entry bookkeeping and the intricacies of the income tax form and at the same time, or soon thereafter, be feminine and helpless when he's in a superior, protective mood. Well, that's the sort of double-entry I can't swing.

Right after retirement he gave up explaining the budget to me. He just handed me his pension and social security checks with a grimly challenging smile. "Here it is," he said. "That's what you've got to go on. You figure it out." And from that moment the responsibility has been mine. I don't say I don't deserve it; if I hadn't gone on so many shopping sprees we might have a little nest egg. But I doubt it. Men go on shopping sprees, too, though they do it with less ardor and fanfare. Ray buys at sales as often as I do, and gets stung worse.

For example, one summer in Pennsylvania he bought a power lawnmower, reduced in price and supersized, from a large friendly store that not only stood behind its merchandise but pushed. The mower flatly refused to cope with our grass. We wrote the store and asked for a refund. We got, instead, an encouraging letter and another lawnmower—same make, same disposition. A second protest brought still another lawn-mower. The manager implied we were simply being difficult. We got lawnmowers and encouraging letters from him all sum-mer. Not a single one of them worked, but I worked; the secre-tarial labor on the project was embittering. It took a lot of energy, but finally all the lawnmowers were returned and we had our money. We also had our grass. Ray still insisted he was right in trying to save by his injudicious buying, even though he had failed, and he implied that the whole thing was my fault.

Then he began rummaging around among his pamphlets.

"It says here," he announced after a long search, "you can control grass if you get a goat."

"You've got a goat," I replied wearily, "but she isn't going to function much longer at this rate."

I can't help thinking I might have missed all the difficulties of budgeting and of buying at sales if I had had a career instead of marriage. I'd have saved lots of money, of course, and I'd have spent it all on myself with no sense of obligation to anybody else. And right now, even at my advanced age, I'd be sunbathing on the Riviera or doing something else equally far-fetched and glamorous. Anyhow, that's what my younger friends tell me, those who haven't been caught in the toils of matrimony (and, believe me, *toils* is the right word!). One of those friends visited me last Tuesday, after I'd sat up half the night figuring out those check stubs.

"My dear," she carolled, "I've just had the most marvelous two weeks in Paris—all sorts of interesting men."

"And you didn't snare one?" I asked, just to be sociable.

"Me, marry? Don't be silly. I'm the head buyer in our department now. What do I want with a husband?"

And she tossed her sables into a corner, narrowly missing my potted geranium. (Things have come to a pretty pass when you're coddling potted geraniums instead of pursuing interesting men.)

It does sort of make one wonder, doesn't it? When she had gone, I tossed my broom into the corner, not having any sables, and sat down to review my miserable life. Here I am, I thought, trying to build a financial empire on a retirement income, and where is it getting me? Ray's okay; he paid only two dollars for our marriage license, so he's made a pretty good investment. Sure, I have a wedding ring, but I also have a bathtub ring, and any hope I had for a career has long since vanished. I would have cried if I hadn't been past the age when a woman looks appealing in tears.

Thank God, I don't often have days like that. Most of the time I am sure that washing diapers and raising sons has been a better deal even than being a head buyer (which sounds rather cannibalistic, anyhow). And I'm convinced now, by sad experience, that a budget in marriage is necessary. It needn't be an absolutely unbreakable one (even the Mosaic laws weren't *that* sturdy!) but it ought to be reasonably firm and unyielding. It's something you get used to in time, like the two-o'clock feeding and walking the dog. I'm also convinced, from sad experience, that the wife should never, never take over the financial reins, unless her husband is a gambler or a pushover who lends money to strangers.

Finance is a man's business. Make him stick with it, even in retirement—especially in retirement. My husband doesn't feel that his virility is undermined in the least by my handling our money, perhaps because there's so little of it left to handle, but for many men a woman's death-grip on the purse would be an insult. They would feel she didn't trust them any more. I'd rather enjoy my husband's feeling that way. I hate to be relied on implicitly, like good old Fido. I wish, once in a while,

Ray would tell me not to bother my pretty head about matters I can't understand. Alas, I married a man who gives me credit for intelligence and the strain is killing me.

Money is not as important in age as faith, health, and friends, but it is certainly next in line. I'm not one of those happy souls who believe that poverty is ennobling. It may be, once in a while, to the very young, but I doubt even that, Abraham Lincoln to the contrary. The old find that poverty is only a humiliation, and it is a humiliation they might have avoided if they'd worried about it in time. The tired, the harassed, the broken in spirit—wouldn't you think able-bodied middle-agers would look at them and rush straight to the bank to open a savings account for their own retirement? Nobody seems able to profit by example, even me.

Ray has told me often that his mother was a financial wizard. (Of course, steak in those days cost a quarter a pound.) She learned from necessity to make all her clothes and his. What *I'd* better learn is to make a reasonable facsimile of a dollar bill. The trouble is, I'm the law-abiding type, and besides, my eyesight is getting too bad for close work.

I hope I haven't given the impression I'm complaining. Ray is, I must admit, a charmingly permissive husband most of the time, glad when I buy a new dress, and always willing to take me out to dinner (especially on the nights frankfurters are scheduled on my menu at home). But I do wish he'd worry a little. As that cheery Mr. Browning used to say, I wish he'd grow old along with me. Right now I'm the one who's getting all the gray hairs.

Oh, well, you can't have everything. Not on a budget.

9

Greener Pastures

There comes a morning when you wake up to find the house has grown too big for you. It has grown too big as children grow—while you weren't looking and had your mind on something else. There you are, you and your husband, like mice in a barn, huddling together for comfort. You've put the extra leaf for the dining room table up in the attic; it's not likely that you'll entertain much at dinner any more, and the children and grandchildren live too far away to visit. Besides, there are the steps. Is it possible you used to run up those steps a dozen times a day without *counting* them?

Then you read in the local paper about the condominium. It's an awful word, and it sounds something like mausoleum, but it's a way of life encouraged by many experts on retirement. You buy your part of a large apartment house, efficiently run by the management. You don't have to bother with upkeep or gardening. You're with a lot of older people who don't have to bother with upkeep or gardening either, and can use all that extra time to visit you, which may or may not have its advantages. You have leisure, lots of it. But lots of leisure is like lots of cayenne pepper or lots of relatives. After a while you may begin to feel that enough is enough.

So the problem becomes simply this: do you want an efficiency apartment with conveniences—or your old house, with memories? There's something to be said for both choices, of course, and the decision depends on individual preference, finances, and health. But, other things being equal, I'd vote for the old homestead every time. Be it ever so humble, I'd rather stay there than in the White House. I *made* it. (Well, my husband and I made it, to be honest.) And I'm not about to hand it over to somebody else, no matter what convenience I get in return. The new tenant would probably let Ray's roses go to seed, and I know she'd repaper the living-room, which Ray did in three different kinds of paper—startling, but somehow nice and cheerful when you got used to it.

I've admitted before that I'm a bad housekeeper, and I intend to go on being a bad housekeeper. I'd be miserable in a condominium. I've had thirty years to battle my untidiness and bully my husband into enduring it, and just now I'm get-

ting into my stride. My house and I play a sort of game together, a game with sentimental overtones, a game that keeps
me from brooding even though it keeps me constantly mad.
Like a remembered nightmare, my house is always escaping
me in bits and pieces—broken knobs on furniture, unmoored
bed slats, cracked egg cups, and spirits of turpentine where
I was sure I had put the vanilla. There's just too much of
it. Think of the hundreds of miles of thread in my spool cabinet. (I treasure a spool cabinet as an archaeologist might treasure the jawbone of a prehistoric animal, for old times' sake.
It belonged to my husband's mother.) Think of the buttons
in my button box. (My husband's mother again.) Think of the
spices and salt and cereal and the millions of particles of dust.
The multitude of things that make up my house baffles and
dazes me. But in an odd way it also comforts me. Surely, surely
no well-meaning spry young neighbor will dare to ask me, in
pitying condescension, what I do all day. I *keep* my house—and
I'd like to see her try it.

Experts on retirement sometimes advise older people to
move into an apartment with no steps to climb, but most doctors agree that stairs are useful in maintaining a healthy heart.
Of course, if your heart is already damaged, or you are getting
actually decrepit, that's a different matter. I refuse to move
into a one-floor apartment for a reason of my own: I would
be a social outcast in a week if I didn't have an upstairs. It
is a valuable asset if you can leave beds unmade all day, giving
them a hurried once-over while your husband is taking his
nightly shower. I do leave beds unmade, even though I know
a finicky friend will drop in for morning coffee and need a
quick trip to the bathroom after the fifth cup. She sprints up
before I can get ahead of her to make the beds. (Curiosity
can make even an octogenarian sprint, if she's female.) She
looks disdainfully at Ray's pajamas on the doorknob and
catches a glimpse of the dog in the middle of my bed. I know
what she's thinking as she comes down those stairs, refreshed
by more than a trip to the bathroom. She's thinking I'm a
slob, which isn't too bright of her, because even a child could
figure that one out. She's also thinking she's a first-rate house-

keeper by comparison and feeling pretty good about it. I may even be invited to attend the next meeting of the Women's Hospital Auxiliary, where, she hints delicately, they need somebody to fold bandages. I don't look smart enough to do anything else.

But I'm smarter than she knows. I'm smart enough not to impose my beloved clutter on a condominium, where I'd have more neighbors close enough to critize me, but with no upstairs to hide in. It would be exactly like living in a hotel, and at my age living in a hotel would make me feel transitory indeed. At any moment a bellhop suspiciously like Gabriel might come in and say, "Check-out time at noon, Madam."

Here in California we have a comfortable home, and here the children lived as adolescents. But I often wish we had never moved from our place in the East, where we lived when they were small. *That* will always be our home place; there is where the toys were put away in the attic one by one. I brought the potty-chair and the duck with me when I moved, and I would have brought all of them if I could. There in the surrounding fields the pets were buried—two dogs, innumerable cats, a rabbit named Hopalong, even one amiable housebroken skunk. Women are sentimentalists; that's one reason for the clutter we live in. But I am less sentimental than most. I can cheerfully throw away old love-letters (though they make good material for blackmail if you keep them long enough). I don't care if I never see my high school annual again. (What was I expecting from life, to look so bright-eyed and naive in that picture with the Woolworth pearls?) But I can't bear to throw away the pink knitted jacket both of my babies wore home from the hospital, and I have kept their first shoes. I don't intend to bronze them; I like the soft feel of them as they were when I used to pinch them to see if they were getting too small. And Ray, as I have said before, would keep his entire past in mothballs if he had room for it.

In the retirement years there isn't a great deal of the future left, so we'd better hang on to the past as much as we can. No important happening of the present can ever be as vivid as the trivialities of those days. I'd rather see the lop-sided horse my son drew on the wall of the bedroom than see the original Mona Lisa herself, with her overrated smile. (She probably would have laughed out loud at that horse!) Psychologists tell us that children ought to stay in one place and put down roots. It is important for parents to stay in one place, too, because their roots are tougher and take hold more slowly. It is the sense of *not belonging* that makes old people seem so aimless and doddering.

A home grows by accretion, as a pearl grows—perhaps even by the stimulus of irritation. It grows day by day, memory by memory. You don't buy it, you create it, and if you're wise you hang on to it, steps or no steps. If it's too large for you to manage, you can close up a few of the rooms. Personally, I have never seen a house too large. How wonderful to have unused space enough for His and Her attics! But if you get desperate you can even rent a room to somebody. This arrangement interferes with privacy, but it's good insurance against not being discovered for three days if you and your husband each break a leg simultaneously. Anyhow, the rent money comes in handy. Indeed it does.

I think it would destroy Ray's self-respect to live near a garden he hadn't made himself. Even quite decrepit old people can garden a little bit. But if you find you can't do it, don't fret about it. If weeds worry you, hire a handyman to plant ground cover. Sow a few perennials, those genial flowers that have sense enough to take care of themselves. Put in a patio of cement or cedar chips; cover bare spots with shrubs and use lots of gravel. Experts in landscaping are quite clever at avoiding the necessity for constant mowing and cultivating. All of this construction involves money, of course, but moving involves money, too, besides a lot of unnecessary regret and heartache. You can't win at this age, but you can at least choose the most comfortable way of losing.

Among the heartaches, if you move into a new apartment, is the necessity of selling or giving away some of your furniture. Did you ever try to do that? It hurts you, because every scar and scratch reminds you of the children, but your husband suffers even more. To most men shabby furniture is like shabby clothes; they nestle into the shabbiness with a relaxed sigh. Ray becomes gloomy if I give away old newspapers.

Moving from the East was a traumatic experience for us. Before Ray left me to take care of the packing job, I told him I was going to get rid of an old chair that had been leaning against the wall of the attic for years. It was an ugly brown color and it was broken in several places. But his face grew pale at my suggestion.

"Give that away? Are you out of your mind? That's the best piece of furniture we've got. Solid pine! I bought it for fifty cents when old man Gile's furniture was auctioned off years ago, and I wouldn't take fifty dollars for it now." He sighed with a sort of weary nostalgia. "They don't make chairs like that any more, or men either. He was a cripple, and he used to sit in front of the coal stove in that chair, warming his feet in the oven. His foot, I mean. Those were the good old days— none of this central-heating nonsense. Don't you dare give it away!"

Well, you see how it goes. Better stay with the things you love—the sofa on which the children lay when they were ill, because you wanted them to be near you in the kitchen; the table that used to be so high their feet didn't touch the floor (it seems small now); and the big double bed in which this whole business started. If you must get rid of some of your treasures, at least keep that bed—and the clock. It has ticked away all the minutes of your marriage—time to warm the bottle for the baby, time to get supper, time to send the boys off to school. Time, time, everlasting and irrevocable time. Not long ago my oldest son phoned me all the way from Pennsylvania, in an unaccustomed mood of homesickness, to tell me under no circumstances to get rid of the clock. I didn't ask him why, but he told me: "I used to lie awake all night Christmas Eve just to hear it strike five. That was the time we always got up to see the tree."

For the wife there remains another distressing problem in house choosing: what will you do if your husband dies? If you have grown children with homes of their own you may be invited, in the generosity of grief, to live with one of them. *Don't do it.* It seems a simple and humane arrangement but the emotional problems involved are almost insoluble. There's no sadder or more misplaced person than a mother trying to make herself useful in a daughter's kitchen, timidly washing the dishes by hand because she's afraid she'll put them wrong-side-in to the dishwasher, getting in the way as she tries to help. She so earnestly *wants* to help, to be kept busy and useful, and when for a moment she can string beans without remembering they're not her business, she is contented. But those interludes are brief; she is rarely allowed to forget she's in her daughter's house: "Mom, let me do that. You go and take a nice nap." Love ought to be able to overcome these small irritations, but love is at its best in big crises, like double pneumonia. So even if you have to take in another woman as a companion, stay in your own home. Accept financial help from your children freely; you've deserved every penny of it. But don't intrude on the life they're building for their own children, a life in which Grandma and Grandpa are devoted but not permanent parts.

Somehow a man whose wife has died fits into a child's home much better than a woman, perhaps because he doesn't have the urge to help with the housework. But the best solution to his problem might be a resident hotel or a convalescent home. Neither one is a *good* solution. Convalescent homes especially are coming under indignant scrutiny by our too-optimistic government. Some of them would make the most hard-boiled social service worker weep. They are the last refuge of the hopeless and the derelict. Sometimes the women inhabitants are set like robots around the television set in the evening, their hair carefully arranged *and their cheeks rouged.* This indignity was visited upon Ray's mother while she was briefly in such a home, and I shudder to think what she would have done had she been able to know what they were doing to *her.* No, a convalescent home isn't a good solution. But there are few good solutions for the retired widow or widower.

Remarriage is a possibility if he or she is still young enough to begin all over again and has the superhuman courage and energy to try. Hollywood is full of elderly people with toupees and masseurs who never give up. But also in the realistic world outside of Hollywood there are people, without toupees and masseurs, who do not find the idea of remarriage ridiculous. And it isn't. It's just a little sad, as well as sweet, like a funeral bouquet. Personally, I can't imagine going into the sunset years with somebody who wasn't with me in the beginning. What about those memories? And how are you going to work off all your frustration on an innocent second husband, who can't possibly know what's bugging you? When you reminisce about poor dead Henry you don't do the new relationship much good, so maybe, all in all, you should skip it.

Near where we live now is a home for the veterans of foreign wars. Ray surely was the most unwarlike of veterans, though to hear him talk you'd think he cut down the enemy without even a bugler to help him. As a matter of honest fact, he was in training camp when peace was declared. But now whenever the going gets tough and the Social Security Administration doesn't sent his check on time he threatens to go to the veterans home. It is a beautiful place, contrary to all expectations, with gardens and game rooms and a taxi service to the nearest bar, which helps mightily when the inhabitants start talking of *their* escapades in battle. They look happy and somewhat contemptuous of the outside world. Now if I can only find a comparable home for the veterans of domestic wars—those fought in the kitchen and bedroom—I'll go there and we can visit on sunny days.

But in the meantime we'll stay in the house where our children have been, full of dust and disadvantages and the sound of running feet. To the professional caretakers of the aged we may seem both stubborn and pitiable, but we'll be happier than they know. And it's *our* business, maybe the last little bit of business we have left.

Anyhow, come to think of it, how can anybody shake the dust mop out of the window of a condominium?

10
The Organization Men

Sometimes—not often—I wish I'd lived in the good old days, when a man's only responsibility was to his conscience and a woman's was to her man. Everything then was straightforward and simple. The economy was run on the barter system: you took your neighbor a chicken and he gave you a mess of vegetables. Later there was the country store, where you leaned over that everlasting cracker barrel to buy from a clerk who called you by your first name and said sure, you could pay him next Tuesday. Now we have supermarkets. You rush down the aisles with a cart, buying more than you need because it's in reach. You wait in line to check out, and you always have one loaf of bread, one measly loaf, on the day when the woman in front of you is buying for a bar mitzvah.

Life is just too complicated, and I don't like complicated things—supermarkets or anagrams or contract bridge or governments. Especially governments. I'm as patriotic as I ought to be, and even a member in good standing of the D.A.R., but I'm getting fed up with bureaucracy. When you retire you're a sitting duck for the Organizers. They move in on you with ghoulish enthusiasm, bringing their blanks and forms and silly questionnaires. The directions for filling these out are confusing and sometimes in fine print, so you get the idea the Organizers hope you'll make a mistake. Maybe they do. If they have to reprocess you because of an error they look busier and more indispensable than ever, and they may even get a raise out of your stupidity. It seems to me that bureaucracy survives on delay, incompetence, and forests. Smoky the Bear ought to start a campaign against the use of trees for making paper. Maybe then we'd have some peace.

My first real brush with bureaucracy came when I tried to get my eighty-year-old mother, who was living with us at the time, into the Medicare program. She didn't have a birth certificate and there seemed to be no way of proving she was past sixty-five. The local office of the Social Security Administration was in a small town about fifteen miles from our home. Although the trip was hard for her to make, I decided I would take her down and introduce her to the young man handling

95

her case. This was direct action, much too direct for the government to tolerate. He was glad to meet her, and shook hands politely, but he insited he needed proof (even though *I* was standing right there).

"Look," I said reasonably, "she's almost too feeble to be sitting up. Can't you make an educated guess that she's reached the Medicare age?"

"No, Ma'm," he answered, with a courtesy that just barely hid a cat-like grin of triumph. "Rules are rules."

Now *that* is a silly statement; a rule can be maneuvered, misinterpreted, twisted, or broken if it's necessary for the good of the cause. No woman worth her salt pays any attention to a man when he says there's no way to get around a man-made rule. But I was too old for the one sure-fire way of getting around it, so I just looked indignant.

"We have to have a signed document," the clerk explained in a pleased way. "How about her wedding certificate?"

That seemed a sensible solution, so we drove fifteen miles back home to get it. If you remember my house—and by now you ought to—you will realize that finding it wasn't easy. My mother misplaces even her false teeth—and anyhow, who wants to keep a wedding certificate after all those years? But I remembered seeing one around somewhere, so I kept searching, and at last I discovered it in my linen closet. (This makes no sense, but it's par for the course.)

We took it fifteen miles back to the interlocutor. He enrolled it and looked gleeful.

"Well, she *was* married—"

Mama spoke up from the well of silence into which she seemed to have dropped.

"Thank you," she said, with icy courtesy. Mama is a Southerner.

"But," the young man added, ignoring her, and leaning forward like a doctor announcing a slow doom, "the date of her birth isn't on the certificate. You should have checked that before you brought it. It just won't do."

"The paper is yellow with age, and the date of her marriage

is on it," I argued desperately. "You might deduce that she was of marriageable age at the time."

"I don't have time for mystery stories, lady," he said. "You'll have to bring me something else."

"All right, I'll bring you something else, but it's going to be my last try." Now *I* leaned forward. "You look like a nice young man. Why don't you get out of here and try to make something of your life?"

"I'm quite happy, thank you. Next, please."

Holding Mama's arm in a fierce protective gesture, I took her back to the car, where my husband was waiting for us.

"Ray, do you know where my birth certificate is?"

"Of course I do," he said. "It's in the safe-deposit box at the bank. If you didn't have me around to take care of things—"

"Skip it. Do you know where the safe-deposit key is?"

Well, that was another matter entirely. When we got home we had to look quite a while for the key. It had slid under a can of soup in Ray's desk drawer. We got the necessary document, drove back fifteen miles, and laid it in front of my friend.

"Now," I said, with a sort of sad triumph, "I'm fifty-eight. This paper proves it beyond a reasonable doubt. So I guess you can sign Mama up for Medicare."

For a moment he looked stunned, as if I had backed him into a corner at last. Then he began to look crafty. Bureaucracy is a crafty business.

"No," he said. "It won't do."

I felt I was in a nightmare, going down a long hot road leading nowhere and battling clouds of mosquitoes as I went. I banged the table with my purse, and all the tired waiting couples in the room seemed interested for the first time since I'd been coming there. Most of the time they had been sitting in torpid dejection, waiting their turn to be told their documentary evidence was lacking. Now they perked up at the hint of tears in my voice.

"Did you hear me?" I yelled, "I'm fifty-eight. If that doesn't prove my mother is at least sixty-five, either you are crazy or I am. And I guess it's me, telling my age to everybody in this room."

Mama, who had insisted on coming along on these expeditions just to see what would happen next, patted my arm. The young man handed me a Kleenex.

"I know it sounds screwy," he admitted. He was sorry for me at last, as well he might have been. I'm sure I looked sixty myself, and Mama looked too perky to be the age she claimed. Excitement was a tonic to her.

"I didn't make the rules," he said soothingly. "The evidence has to concern your mother, not you. Was she ever confined in a hospital?"

"Yes, oh yes," Mama said, pushing me aside so she could get closer to the desk. "It wasn't when my babies were born; I'm an old-fashioned woman and always was, so I had my babies at home, which is right and proper. All this mollycoddling in hospitals is ridiculous, and how do you know you've got your own child back? I think—"

"Mama, please. Answer the question."

"What question?" she said vaguely, overcome suddenly with the timidity and forgetfulness of age. I led her to one of the empty chairs and went back into the battle.

"She had an operation in Pennsylvania when she was seventy-six, at the Norristown Hospital."

"Good, good!" My prosecutor was on my side now. I thought he might grab me and kiss me; it would have been a hearty grandmotherly kiss, and I would have deserved it. "That ought to do it. Get a record from the hospital, dated, and she's in."

I was so happy I forgave him my aching head and feet, but as I was leaving I couldn't help giving him a little jolt, something to think about when he had a moment or two free from poring over questionnaires and keeping his rules and regulations unblemished.

"Women lie a lot about their age," I said gently. "How does the Social Security Administration know her age on the hospital record is right? She was the one who gave it to them, don't you remember?"

He looked over at Mama, sitting with her hands in her lap, child-like and waiting.

"She's one of them that wouldn't lie," he said, with a reproachful smile. He had won after all. I left the office feeling guilty and ashamed.

That, so help me, is the unvarnished truth. There is very little common sense left in the government; it has got too big and too bossy. The paper work necessary to run even a crossroads hamlet is staggering. Ray hates bureaucracy as much as I do, and the day he wrestles with his income tax is always a black one in our household. But he isn't averse to a little do-it-yourself bureaucracy at home. I've never seen anybody so addicted to files. He is convinced that life—even life with me—will fall easily into its proper pattern if you just make lists.

He keeps all his addresses on cards and has a heavy wooden cabinet full of them—the address of the people who lived next door when he was a boy, and that of the man who gave him a bum market tip in 1928, and even that of a girl who once sent him a Christmas tie by mistake. He cherishes these outmoded records so lovingly it takes a lot of research to find a current card when it is needed. His concern over them is a touching indication of his need to hold on to the past.

He also writes notes to himself on little cards and leaves them on his desk: "Mail box to Clarence, get piece of lumber for shelf, dental appointment." One day he saw me looking too critically at one of these reminders, and the next day I found a cryptic note: "One extra-dry martini, one blond 36x24x36." All I can say is, that blond will need the extra-dry martini.

Even grocery lists, my husband insists, should be made on cards. I have never figured that one out. Perhaps he intends to keep on permanent file the record of my extravagances, but I think he's just got into the filing habit and can't quit, like all those other bureaucrats. I make lists, too, but never on filing cards. Like any other self-respecting female I make them on the backs of old envelopes, or on the edges of newspapers, or even on the backs of other lists (which is, I guess, compounding a felony). Moreover, the lists are usually cryptic, like "pot. and mt.," which any idiot ought to understand if he's seen the inside of a kitchen. But not Ray. "What, my dear," he asks severely, "do you intend to do with a pot and a mountain? I don't want to seem uncooperative, but I'll say this—if you worked for our government they'd have to close up the shop."

"I want potatoes and meat," I answer. "By now you ought to know. As for doing government work—ha! I'd rather starve."

Then I get a lecture on tidiness, a sense of responsibility, and definiteness (what kind of meat?). I can't win. Nobody lets me alone to work out my own salvation. I think I could do it, too. But maybe I couldn't: maybe I need to be taken over and organized. Whether I need to or not, that seems to be the fate in store for me. We are entering the age of computers, and I rather wish I'd been born in another era. Enough is enough. I can endure Ray's meddling with my various inadequacies; after all, it's the most stimulating hobby in marriage after the honeymoon has worn off. What I can't endure is being chided by a machine, because I can't fight back. I am baffled even by a can opener, which leaves half the lid on no matter how I work it.

The whole concept of automation frightens me. It's bad enough to be out of work because you've reached sixty-five—a vigorous, defiant, competent, but nevertheless useless sixty-five. It's tragic to be out of work when you're young, just because you're made of flesh and blood instead of steel. As the wife of a retired man who is desperate for something to do, I petition civilization to stop where it is and go no further. Scientists are even experimenting with the creation of life in test tubes. Soon husbands, nice as they are, will be obsolete. Man has a stubborn way of outsmarting himself, and he's about to do it again.

Pretty soon Ray's wooden file cabinet will be obsolete, too, as well as his sense of independence and his joy in the past.

All our vital information will be cherished by the government and kept on postage-stamp microfilm; we won't have to do a thing about life except endure it and fill up those confounded leisure hours. We will die in democratic anonymity and our ashes will be stored in a numbered vault. No wonder men are investigating space; there's *got* to be some place where the wheel hasn't yet been invented.

The computers even try match making, though so far that kind of nonsense seems to be reserved for television audiences. A man and woman are analyzed and the results fed into a machine. After a very short time—just about long enough for the participants to shake hands—the answer comes out of a slot. It is, at least on television, a cold, uncompromising affirmative, so we assume the marriage takes place, perhaps in a boiler room, and the couple live happily ever after with a house full of mechanical gadgets contributed by a grateful C.B.S. Now I may be old-fashioned, but I'd like at least a modicum of romance in the show. Couldn't somebody paint a Cupid on the computer or play *Hearts and Flowers* over the intercom? I suppose it is naive to imagine that anyone really gets married after one of these performances, but the premise is so shocking it should never be presented to the world. (Of course, divorce under such circumstances would be easy: you could always blame it on a short-circuit.)

Even books and magazines try to organize and classify us; they are full of pompous probings that would make us feel abjectly helpless if we took them seriously. We can't have a single opinion of our own, subversive or otherwise, and keep it private; and I maintain that to be subversive in secret is not only invigorating but good for the soul. The journalistic Peeping Toms have taken over. Our political affiliations, our stand on war and peace and racial problems, our reaction to streaking, our libidos—everything is examined and tabulated. I don't know what the examiners are trying to prove—perhaps the simple fact that we are sheep. We never get a good rousing story in the magazines any more; we just get good rousing surveys. We're invited to take tests to determine whether we are good drivers, or good citizens, or good husbands and wives—and whose business is it, I'd like to know? Of course, we don't *have* to take the tests, but when there's nothing else to do. . . .

I admit I'm a pushover for that last test. Now that the course is almost run, I have a neurotic compulsion to look back and see where I went off the track. Such knowledge won't do me a bit of good; it may even be painful. But I answer the list of silly questions anyhow, as one puts pressure on an aching tooth.

I saw a questionnaire like that the other day and spent a confusing hour trying to decide whether I should have married or instead gone into thermodynamics, a career that looked a lot easier when I got through my soul searching.

"Are you," the interrogator asked, "a companion to your husband in his leisure hours?" Well, looking back, I can see that he had quite a few, off and on, but I don't remember that I had a single one till the children left home. How could I have been his companion? (Who thinks these questions up? Not a woman, I'll bet.) Now that we're older we get rather tired of each other in our leisure hours. We have too many of them.

"Do you laugh at your husband's jokes?" No, I don't. He used to save his really good ones for his boss on the golf course. Our private family jokes were on the distressing side, and concerned catastrophes like the time I served a nearly raw chicken to his best friend, in my salad days. (Salads I could do, even as a bride.)

"Are you a tidy housekeeper?" When I read that one, I just sat and cried for a while.

"Are you economical?" Alas, not very, and I never was. In the beginning I figured I ought to be paid somehow for my housekeeping chores, and the best way seemed to be to add a dollar to the price of steak and pocket the difference. It wasn't a commendable technique, and I'm sorry for it now.

"Are you good-natured?" You bet I am. If I weren't, I'd be serving time in San Quentin right now and Ray would still be running toward Alaska. But this is the only question I passed, absolutely the only one. I failed the others and scored only ten on the whole thing.

I was, in fact, in such a humble mood I made a kettle of clam chowder for Ray's supper. He ate it with surprise and gusto, but after the last mouthful was swallowed he said it somehow didn't taste like the kind his mother used to make.

"It doesn't," he said wistfully, "seem to have any clams in it. You must be getting absentminded. I read a survey the other day on the attention span of the elderly. . . ."

See what I mean? You can't win.

11

Just Keep
An Eye
On Junior

I have found that one of the most distressing aspects of my own retirement—which came simultaneously with my husband's—is what might be called the Mother's Helper syndrome. The active and young decide that you aren't able to enjoy life any more, what with your rheumatism and the dentures that don't fit, so you might as well help them enjoy it. You sit on the sidelines, but you sit there with a baby on your lap, or a skein of knitting, or the neighbor's cat. Or, worse than these, the minutes of the last meeting. You are always called upon to be secretary of the innumerable clubs you join in the hope that they will make some of the loneliness go away. And you are *grateful* for any job you get. That's the awful part of the deal. You are grateful.

My own philanthropic activities, which I didn't think of myself, are conducting rummage sales and baby-sitting. I used to be elected secretary of stimulating groups like International Relations, where I was instrumental in getting good-looking foreign diplomats to speak. But that was in my glamorous middle-age. Now that I am a gray-haired grandmother they ask me to be chairman of the rummage sale, and they ask it so nicely I haven't the heart to refuse.

"Gee, I hope you can help us out. We need someone like you with lots of experience. You aren't really busy these days, are you?"

"No," I say. "Everything I had to do was finished years ago."

And it was, my dear. I positively look forward to that rummage sale and to the mountains of torn undershirts and worn-out socks I will be sorting. Anything is better than staying home. Besides, once I found a cut-glass sugar bowl in the debris and bought it for thirty-five cents, a piece of skullduggery that compensated for my tired feet and bruised heart.

But, to tell the bitter truth, I am tired of being helpful. I would like, just once more, to be interesting and selfish, to be young and even gossiped about. This is a secret pleasure, this dream of suddenly losing all one's gray hair and inhibitions in one fell swoop, and turning into a *femme fatale* before the world's astounded eyes. No woman believes she's old. She doesn't believe it in spite of her chairmanship of the rummage sale. This, I think, is one of the nicest—and saddest—facts of life, and one that should be told to Junior along with the story of the birds and the bees. He'll be a better husband for it. A confused husband, no doubt, but a better one.

Because I dress circumspectly, if not dowdily, and so far have refused to wear a much-needed wig, nobody suspects me of wanting to be a *femme fatale.* Nobody knows, not even my hairdresser. I am, however, often accused of being tough-minded and prickly with prejudices, an accusation that is wholly false. Ask any of my friends. I am so full of the milk of human kindness I'm soggy. Just let any young mother look doleful and immediately I offer to baby-sit while she goes out to tea (or whatever she goes out to, and I don't think it's always tea). I don't want to offer, but I do. I'm expected to. And, as I said before, in my inmost heart I am grateful, though my common sense may reject the idea.

"I don't like to be any trouble," she says, "You can sit here in the living room if you like and read. But just keep an eye on Junior. Sometimes he walks in his sleep."

That's what I get when I baby-sit—babies who won't sit, or even lie down. I get the sleep-walkers and those with nightmares. I get children who aren't toilet-trained and forget all their inhibitions when I take them on my lap. I get children who sneak out of the bedroom and give a war-whoop that shakes me up for the rest of the evening. Or I get children who beg me for stories.

I told my own children fairy stories. But a quite different interpretation of fairies is abroad in the land, so I keep quiet and settle for Mother Goose. Having reached the age of retirement and, presumably, reason, I think Mother Goose is silly now. I have never understood her popularity—except, of course, that children are pretty silly, too, at a tender age. (But, as Lawrence Welk would say in another context, "Wonderful, wonderful!")

Once, in desperation, I revised a few of her verses and tried them out on the kids. They went something like this:

Pussycat, pussycat, where have you been?
I've been to London to look at the Queen.
Pussycat, pussycat, what saw you there?
I saw a little mouse under a chair.
Pussycat, pussycat, why the big grin?
The mouse was under the chair she was in.

And the children, completely ignoring my literary effort, went on something like this:
"Did you ever see a mouse?"
"Certainly, darling. Go to sleep."
"Is there a mouse under this chair?"
"Of course there isn't. Go to sleep."
"Are you sure? I think I hear a funny sound."
"I tell you there's no mouse under this chair. If you don't go to sleep—"
"You get up and let's see if there's a mouse under this chair."
So I get up, and there's no mouse under the chair, and I wish I had kept my darn mouth shut. But my questioner is just getting into her stride.
"Well, let's look in the bedroom, and the kitchen, and Dad's den, and the attic." By this time the little vixen is wide awake, slightly scared, and completely happy. And I am committed to a room-by-room survey of my neighbor's house, an adventure I might enjoy if I weren't in a position of trust and responsibility.
So I open the book again.

Jack be nimble, Jack be quick,
Jack jump over the candlestick.
The fire department is feeling sick.

Well, this distracts the child from the mouse, but only temporarily appeases her. She sighs in a pleased and thoughtful manner.
"I had candles for my birthday. Want to see me blow one out?"

"Not now, honey. It's time to go to bed."

"I just gave one big blow and there they went. If the electricity went off, would you light a candle?"

"I expect I would."

"Let's turn it off. I know where the switch is."

"What would your father say to that?"

"He'd say Mama forgot to pay the bill again."

By now I am beginning to realize this child is too big to cope with, and I certainly ought not to be rocking her, so I slide her off my lap. She clutches me and gets right back to the mouse.

"I hear it, I hear it! I don't want to go to bed!"

So I let her sit up a while longer, for fear she'll howl. I always get kids who howl. That's why their mothers go out so much.

As I remember them under such circumstances, my two sons were angels. But that is hindsight. In my saner moments I know they were normal, unreasonable children, and I reared them to manhood by the grace of God and Dr. Spock, not necessarily in that order. Ray got along with them much better than I did. In spite of his impatience with nearly everything—lost buttons, untidy cupboards, and irresponsible women—he is tender and patient with children. I think it is because he feels safe when he is with them, as well as honored. They don't ask him to sign papers or fill out blanks, they don't tell him he is too old for the job, they just listen to his imaginative stories, cuddle close, and accept. Is that perhaps what we're supposed to do with Father Time—cuddle and accept?

Unfortunately, it was impossible for Ray to accept retirement. He looked for a job here in California as soon as we arrived, and he got one in a real estate office. But it didn't last long. He has quite definite ideas about houses and he dislikes the slipshod variety that dot the California landscape, so he was never happy with any that he sold. One day I heard him talking to a prospective tenant on the phone. "That place you want belonged to a couple who liked dogs and kept them in the house. It smells terrible, but I'll take you out for a look at it if you like." Of course they declined, and Ray was fired the next day with genuine regret. His employer said he was simply too honest to be a salesman.

At seventy-six he is now a chemist in a winery owned by a family that doesn't care what age their workmen are as long as they can stand up. That is a literal requirement; no chair or stool is allowed in the laboratory. But Ray doesn't mind. What's a little thing like standing on your feet all day when you plan to start jogging at any moment?

12

Between
The Dark
And The
Daylight

If in this discussion I have seemed to touch with unbecoming frivolity on the problems of the retired man and his wife, it's because a sense of humor, misplaced as it may be, is the only thing that makes the subject tolerable. I truly laugh that I may not weep. Think of it: after standing wearily in line, on feet that hurt, to fill in blanks for Social Security and Medicare, we realize we've still got the biggest blank of all to fill—the years ahead. Robert Browning once remarked, in a cheerful mood, that the last part of life is the best, the part for which the first was made. All I can say about this fatuous bit of optimism is that poets are among the few people who keep their jobs until the bitter end. Most of us get along the best we can, picking up a little sustenance here and there, trying to ignore the fact that we are in a spiritual if not an actual bread line.

Under the present Social Security law, retirement is made unnecessarily difficult for the man who has only a small pension or none at all. He can't get a well-paid extra job and still get his government check until he is seventy-two and presumably too feeble to work at all. Lately Social Security payments have been raised several times to keep up with inflation, and President Ford has discussed the problems of the aged with representatives of the Gerontological Society, the American Home Nursing Association, the American Association of Retired Persons, and similar groups. This increased interest in our older people is encouraging, but it is not enough. They are still the step-children of society.

It is difficult to keep up one's morale in such a situation. Here is where the wife comes into the picture again. A woman is more given to remembering than a man. It is she who keeps the pressed roses and the ribbons from the prom bouquet. She builds for herself a pleasant mental retreat into which she can retire when the roast burns, the bills pile up, and her bifocals are broken for the fourth time in a year. In that retreat she learns to ignore the disastrous present and to concentrate on happier times, living over again her first kiss, her first baby, and the shining commitment she made to marriage when

115

burnt roasts and bifocals weren't even in her mind. This escapism is peculiarly feminine and self-preserving, and she should try to share it with her husband.

I am sure some retired men idealize the past, just as a woman tends to do, seeing themselves as giants of industry struck down before their time by the pebbles of bureaucracy. But I suspect that most of them, at a certain age, have a pervasive sense of failure. A sense of failure comes easily to a man, because his standards are down-to-earth, practical, and in most cases monetary. In one thing only does his dream-life approximate a woman's: he treasures his virility and mourns its passing. That, to me at least, explains why gray-haired church deacons often run away with chorus girls, and I can't always blame them as much as the Good Book says I should. Man's wistful summing up of lost chances is one of the favorite themes of poetry, from Leight Hunt's *Jenny Kissed Me* to Dylan Thomas's resentful and beautiful elegy to his father.

What can you do with a man who sees his whole life as a mess just because he's turned sixty-five? Well, you can brain-wash him. It isn't easy, but it's a better use of psychology than the Communists ever thought up. Tell your husband he's been a fine helpmeet and father; tell him over and over, both obliquely and directly, in both teasing and serious moods. When your marriage has been a good one, this follow-up therapy works almost at once; when it has been a bad one—and there are bad marriages, plenty of them—it is an act of grace. Look back and accentuate the positive in whatever kind of marriage you have had. Maybe the bad times weren't as terrible as they seemed at the time. When you're sixty-five and past, you would spend your life with a robot in jail just to be young again.

Whatever doubts may plague you personally, try to stop your husband's compulsive second-guessing. You know the gloomy procedure. He stands at the window and watches the rain—a rain the crops need but he doesn't, and he mumbles: "It was wrong to leave that job in Ohio. We've moved too much. . . . I would have got that contract in 1952 if Howard had kept his word. . . . Maybe we shouldn't have had kids, they just cause trouble. . . . You sort of liked that guy you met before we married, didn't you? Bet he's made his pile by now. . . . My God, woman, don't you ever wash these windows?"

Stop this nonsense at once. You can stop it by getting mad and telling *him* to wash the windows, but the best answer is to do a little gentle reminiscing of your own: "Do you remember the hunting trip you took with the boys? It meant a lot to them; they've told me so. . . . I was looking at our wedding pictures today. You haven't changed a bit!"

This is pure altruism, and it succeeds. Your husband will straighten his shoulders and maybe even shine his shoes. And perhaps he will give you the final accolade:

"This darn government is making a mistake, letting competent men go to waste. I could tell those dimwits in Washington a few things if I had a chance."

"Why don't you, dear?" you ask gently, knowing in your heart he would have no more influence than a fly. "You ought to go there for a few days, just by yourself. You need the trip."

"Say, that's an idea! Sure you don't want to come along?"

You ignore the lack of enthusiasm in his invitation and assure him you can't possibly leave home now; there are all those beans to can, and besides, you get a little nervous on planes (an understatement of governmental magnitude). So he goes alone, and he doesn't upset the bureaucrats one bit, which to my way of thinking is a shame. But he enjoys the pretty girls and the mini-skirts and takes a side trip to pay his respects to the Statue of Liberty, an old friend who seems to have forgotten he's around. And in due course you get the postcard you've been waiting for: "Wish you were here."

I should like to add a postscript about the final enemy to contented old age—fear. I'm not talking about the fear of illness, which we can usually face with equanimity in this antibiotic age, or even the fear of loneliness, which we can somehow survive. But sometimes we wake in the night to a deeper fear, the fear of decrepitude, of not being able to cope even with so small a venture as crossing the street, of simply falling apart—the fear, in short, of death. If we can reach out to somebody, we feel momentarily reassured. If this person is a loved one who has laughed at our bogeymen before, we may go back to sleep again. And we may not—

It is said that young medical students often become howling hypochondriacs from the burden of knowledge they bear; their own bodies, taken for granted before, are revealed to them as such staggering miracles that they collapse at the sight. They are lost in the pattern of bones and arteries, the clever checks and balances, the steady heart that has already beaten more times than they can count but could erase the world if it stopped for only a moment. It is all a miracle, poised on a hair; death is as close and as real as life. It is the miracle in reverse. They can, and do, measure the human brain; they touch it on the postmortem table, wondering perhaps why it doesn't throw off sparks and light up the room instead of lying there in terrifying inertness. How can a gray lump of matter hold the songs of Shakespeare, the mathematics of Euclid and Einstein, and all human emotions from hate to reverence?

We don't have to be medical students to react violently to this image. It is better, of course, not to think at all about mortality, but try and ignore it when the little warning signals of pain and weariness begin! We burrow into our pillows and watch the window for dawn, doubting that we'll last till then. And as we lie there we review the past, mourning not so much our failure to *do* as our failure to *see*. What happened to the good, sound days, with their sunrises and sunsets? Twenty-four hours in every one of them, and we didn't notice. And now we're going to be called to account at any moment. If only the sun would come up for us, just one more time!

This sort of thinking is foolishness, but it is human, and our sufferings in the night are real. For we know from long experience that nobody wins the game; it is always decided in favor of the House. Humanity conquers the black plague, and gets the atom bomb. We learn to live in compassionate unity with each other, and get bureaucracy. We are given a fine brain with which to think, and we think about death.

I don't know how to conquer fear. Everyone must work it out for himself. The conventionally religious will go to the Bible: "I will lift up mine eyes to the hills, from whence cometh my help." The operative words here are "lift up." It is the inward looking that destroys us. Some may find more comfort in poetry than in religion—not the brash nihilism of the moderns but the solid faith of the old-timers who used to reassure our parents from the pages of McGuffey's readers: Tennyson, Browning, Landor, Bryant, all of whom faced the end of things with courage and tranquillity. Old Landor said it with grace and brevity: "I warmed both hands before the fire of life; it sinks, and I am ready to depart."

For some stubborn and unorthodox reason I am helped most by Christ's human cry as he died: "My God, my God, why hast thou forsaken me?" It is hard for me to pity God's son, but very easy to pity Mary's—and if He could feel despair even temporarily, who am I to be ashamed of mine?

Well, it all comes down to this: we can't understand the Plan, supposing there is one; we are stumblers and doubters to the end, no matter how hard we try to be otherwise. That we have run the hard course without fainting, and married and borne children, must surely be counted in our favor. We have helped Him in the unceasing act of creation; perhaps He will help us, forgiving our human errors because they rise out of human needs. At least we can remember we are not wholly lost as long as we keep faith with love or the memory of love.

Perhaps the best picture of the retirement years is that of a man and woman looking backward without regret and forward without fear, laughing a little at life and at themselves.

13
Epilogue For Oldsters
Double Bedlam

The subject of retirement is so dreadful to contemplate that I refuse to end this discussion on a serious note. But I'd better end it, and soon; Ray says, if it's ever published I'll have to use a pseudonym, preferably Arabic. So one more bit of advice, and I'll exit smiling (at least outwardly).

I've decided, after all the research I've done on our marriage and others, that one of the worst problems facing older people is beds. Yes, beds—plain ordinary beds. Don't underrate them. A plain ordinary cold may turn into pneumonia, and a plain ordinary bed may have equally disastrous consequences, not necessarily obstetrical. It's difficult for me even to *spell* that word at my age, much less have any truck with it, as my grandmother used to say. She had twelve children, and she had gathered a lot of information about beds, here and there, but she had never had even half a chance to consider the question I now propose: shall we Golden Agers sleep comfortably in single ones, or companionably in double ones? Grandpa had the answer. So, from a somewhat different point of view, had Ray. He had it long before he met me (and I blame that, like everything else, on his mother).

He reserved twin beds for our honeymoon, a fact of life I didn't know about (and didn't want to know about, either). I was struck dumb with consternation. When I had got over my initial shock and a good fit of crying he explained that he could never sleep with anyone, man or woman, because his partner always hogged most of the space and all of the blankets. He had never practiced with me, so how had he come by this bit of esoteric information? I wanted to cry again, but I feared a runny nose wasn't going to be conducive to romance, if any, on this trip, so I kept quiet. And contemplative. As a matter of fact, I sleep diagonally in a bed, which does make companionship difficult but doesn't interfere with other aspects of marriage. Anyhow, when you're on your honeymoon it's not considered cricket to sleep, diagonally or otherwise. If you do, you don't mention it in your memoirs. So if your husband dares to suggest twin beds at any time in your marriage, from the honeymoon to the last rites, go straight home to mother. And while you're there you might ask her to explain the facts of life all over again. You must have missed a point somewhere.

First of all, separate beds lead insidiously to separate rooms and separate baths. I resent the separate baths. Do I have athlete's foot? Do I have whatever it is your best friends won't tell you about? No, I do not. I have only a husband who likes to keep himself to himself, perhaps hoping to dodge a woman bent on rearranging things. His bath is clean, tidy, and personal. He has stacks of extra Kleenex and bathroom tissue on the floor, ready for any emergency, and he has a small cabinet full of eye drops, iodine sprays, toothpicks and other masculine accessories, including a toothpaste simply brimming with fluoride, which he swears is good for any cavity, even in the floor. (And, darn him, every tooth he has is perfect, while I fear mine may fall in the soup at some inauspicious moment, like at a luncheon of the D.A.R.) BUT he squeezes this toothpaste tube from the bottom! That alone makes him a suspect in my mind; if he does that, he will soon begin to look under my carpets and on top of my refrigerator for evidences of sloth.

My bathroom has mouldy stacks of glamor magazines, an ancient scale that weighs ten pounds lighter than it should and is worth its weight in gold, and a lot of half-used perfumes and discarded lipsticks, all of which I've tried and none of which has done me any good. But I squeeze my toothpaste tube at random here and there, and often leave the top off. That, in my estimation, proves I'm a perfectly normal woman.

When I was young and unmarried and hopeful I spent a lot of money on fancy nightgowns, God knows why. Now I wear mismatched pajamas, sometimes wrong-side out. Who sees me, anyhow? When I do find myself, to my surprise, in an outfit without holes that looks positively decent, I hope the house will catch on fire. We've got insurance. *Then* Ray might notice me—but come to think of it, I haven't any insurance on that. Anyhow, I hope nobody would notice him. He has been hanging on to a flannel bathrobe so tattered it barely covers him; when I meet him in the hall at night I shudder. He says he likes it because his illustrious mother gave it to him and it's warm. It may be, in the few spots where it touches him.

Well, let him go down the drain if it pleases him; I still try, once in a while, to remember that I'm a very attractive woman for my age. That's what the salesgirl told me last Wednesday when she sold me, over my feeble protests, a black chiffon negligee for forty dollars. Then she added, coyly, "We have to keep at it, don't we?"—a remark that somehow dimmed her compliment considerably, and made me feel like a vampire with a bank account. But the next morning I felt like a somewhat overdone Zsa Zsa Gabor as I strolled into the room where Ray was eating breakfast. He glanced up and announced that the weatherman predicted rain. Then he noticed I was different. "Oh," he asked, "in mourning for somebody?" His sense of humor lies pretty low till his third cup of coffee. "Yes," I said, aching inside. "I am. Myself." Then I added spitefully, "I bought this little wraparound for forty dollars, and I'm not going to take it back."

"My mother," he mused, "used flannel nightgowns. They were very warm. It gets cold in New England."

"Nothing like as cold as it gets here. In the rest of the house it's about nine below, and I suspect you'd freeze into immobility in the bedroom."

Ray looked puzzled and a little worried. He has never understood me; I'd better be glad he never will.

"Turn up the thermostat, why don't you?" he suggested. But I turned up the flame under the frying pan instead and cooked his egg to a hard lump that even a camel couldn't digest. A woman can't take everything.

This summer we went on a weekend visit to a friend who innocently provided us with a double bed. Ray looked disgruntled and confused, as if he'd stumbled into the wrong Pullman berth and found an amazon woman inside.

"Look here," he said, "I forgot to bring my pajamas. Remember when we flew East to see the kids and I forgot my shorts? I seem to have done it again. Do you suppose I'm getting old? What'll I do?"

That was a double-barrelled question, but I had the answer to both barrels.

"Get in bed with me," I suggested, trying to sound offhand about it.

But he just stood there in that sleazy bathrobe and shook his head.

"Damn it," he said, "I'm *embarrassed.*"

I decided then and there that a man who is embarrassed over nakedness after thirty years of marriage needs a little therapy, like a frying pan thrown at his head. But I kept calm. "Get in, Ray, and stop that shivering. It's reasonable to suppose you'll sleep warmer with *something*, if it's only a shaggy dog." So, comforted by this logic, he got in—and I slept diagonally, vertically, horizontally, and bitterly all night long.

We don't make up our beds alike, either. He does his before breakfast, because he says I never do it right, although he's demonstrated his technique often. The bottom sheet must be exactly one inch from the headboard, the top sheet two inches below, and all the covers tucked in at the bottom of the bed. When he's through it looks as if he's just made a particularly cozy coffin. I make my bed in a frenzy, for neither sheets nor blankets come out right, and I don't tuck in the covers at all, so I can get out at either the top or the bottom, which comes in handy if the house *does* catch fire. Consequently, the whole affair looks as if somebody slept in it all day. And I often do, when life with a retired husband—a *very* retired husband—literally gets me down.

But I love him—who else would have put up with me all these years?

126